TENNESSEE
WILLIAMS
101

TENNESSEE
WILLIAMS
101

AUGUSTIN J CORRERO

PELICAN PUBLISHING
NEW ORLEANS 2021

The word "Pelican" and the depiction of a pelican are trademarks of Arcadia Publishing Company Inc. and are registered in the U.S. Patent and Trademark Office.

Library of Congress Cataloging-in-Publication Data

Names: Correro, Augustin J., author.
Title: Tennessee Williams 101 / Augustin J. Correro.
Description: New Orleans : Pelican Publishing, 2021.
| Includes bibliographical references and index. |
Summary: "A Tennessee Williams biography written
for newcomers and old fans wanting to learn more
about the playwright and the world he built"—
Provided by publisher.
Identifiers: LCCN 2020052251 | ISBN 9781455625345
(paperback) | ISBN 9781455625352 (Ebook)
Subjects: LCSH: Williams, Tennessee, 1911-1983. |
Dramatists, American—20th century—Biography.
Classification: LCC PS3545.I5365 Z6148 2021 | DDC
812/.54 [B]—dc23
LC record available at https://lccn.loc.gov/2020052251

Cover illustration by Augustin J Correro.

Printed in the United States of America
Published by Pelican Publishing
New Orleans, LA
www.pelicanpub.com

For Nick, who has encouraged and held space for my many nerdoms—animals, comic books, and, surely chief among them, the life and works of Tennessee Williams

Contents

DRAGON COUNTRY

Tennessee Williams' Mythic Mississippi Delta

Moon
Lake

TIGER TAIL
COUNTY

Cypress Hill
Cemetery

Clarksdale

Laurel

Straw
Plantation

Meighan
Plantation

Rosedale

TWO RIVER
COUNTY

Grenada

Blue Mountain

Glorious Hill

Moony's Lot

Greenwood

Winona

Greenville

Indianola

Bethesda

GREENE
COUNTY

MISSISSIPPI

Witch's Bayou

Rolling Fork

Yazoo City

Introduction

A LEGEND

Once upon a time, a passing knowledge of America's greatest playwright Tennessee Williams could be taken for granted. *A Streetcar Named Desire* or *The Glass Menagerie* was on high school reading lists across the United States, and many literature surveys in colleges would touch on Williams, too. Over the past couple of decades, Williams' plays have been edged out of curricula in favor of other material. Today, it's mostly theatre classes that truck in Williams' work, and even that's not a given. His life and legacy are increasingly becoming "niche" knowledge. Specialized. Arcane.

Several years ago, I was first asked to start giving Tennessee Williams 101 presentations at Williams-themed events. No, not Williams-themed bachelorette parties or Renaissance Faire-style villages (although, if you can find a market for that, I'd go). A handful of literary and theatre festivals have cropped up since the playwright's death, and as his life story became more obscured by time, the festivals wanted a primer. That's where I came in. I would cram the life and works of Williams and his significance to the American theatre into approximately an hour. The presentation wasn't just for Williams nerds like me, though. It's for everyone: die-hard fans, drama students on class trips, Southern lit scholars cooling their heels between salons and panels, the spouses of the aforementioned groups, and those daring townies trying the festivals on for size.

The live-in-living-color Tennessee Williams 101 has the same aim as this book: explaining Williams to the contemporary audience and smashing the museum case that has crept up and encircled a truly fascinating man. When I present and—I hope—as I put these words down, my aim is to convey the magnificent, messy, and completely relatable story of a small-town kid who defied odds to make an indelible impact on the artistic landscape of the twentieth century.

But how does one adequately explain Tennessee Williams in a handy, portable handbook? The three most famous plays he wrote are each more pages than the volume you hold, and they only account for an infinitesimal percentage of his gross creative product! He wrote a lot. Like, a lot, a lot. We have more writings available to us by Tennessee Williams than any other American writer of note. Between poems, plays, short stories, novellas, essays, and the hundreds of letters, notebooks, journals, and other odds and ends that have surfaced—published and unpublished—it's fair to say Williams had a compulsion to write. That's why we have a panoramic view of his life: both exterior and interior.

Williams created a world full of curiosities and contradictions, all for the purpose of giving his audience a better view of themselves and each other. The world he imagined seemed connected to ours, but parallel. It was a little bit wilder. So that's where I'll take you. For you, my goal is to present a complete view from the ground level. As the country he wrote about was magical and familiar, it's not a handbook that's needed at all, but an atlas. We will travel down the back roads of this wild country conceived by Tennessee Williams, taking in the sights, getting to know the locals, and breathing the rarified air. It's this world that Tennessee Williams lovers enjoy inhabiting for fleeting moments shared with the page and the stage. Maybe once you've covered the map, you'll want to live there, too.

And what's a map without a . . .

LEGEND

The chief biographical facts and figures are laid out periodically through the chapters as **Points of Interest** for an easy-to-follow timeline, broken up into segments. These points are elaborated on in the narrative, which focuses on Williams' development as a writer and his lived experience. Here's a worthy set to begin with.

Points of Interest

- Tennessee Williams is an American playwright who lived from 1911 to 1983.
- Williams is best known for writing *The Glass Menagerie, A Streetcar Named Desire,* and *Cat on a Hot Tin Roof.*
- He wrote over 100 plays of varying length and about as many poems.
- He also wrote novellas, essays, screenplays, and dozens of short stories. And, he painted.
- For his contributions to American drama and literature, he was awarded with Drama Desk Awards, a Tony Award, two Pulitzer Prizes, the Presidential Medal of Freedom, and others.

You'll also find, boldfaced so as not to mix them up with the cold hard facts, several **Detours.** The Points of Interest are the connecting dots for our roadmap of the subject's life, then the narrative develops details, illustrating the corners and crevasses that should be explored. The detours provide some context or connection to the world in which the subject moved and continues to move— our world. Sometimes they'll elaborate on ideas that are easy to overlook, or offer a contemporary lens through which to view the material. They delve into what I've experienced to be valid arguments or additions to the conventional wisdom of Williams' life and works. I've been careful to mark the beginnings and **ends of these detours.**

For the supremely nerdy Easter-egg hunters like me, some chapters end with a note on the SCENIC ROUTE, which expands on material featured in the narrative or detours for those who like to dive down rabbit holes.

Finally, I've included a **Q&A** section, inspired by some actual questions I have commonly been asked at in-person presentations. Additionally, I have included **Appendices** that delve more deeply into complex topics—mostly theatrical—that may seem too dense or specialized for the "strictly 101," but I hope might delight you anyway!

You may also observe: this text uses the Broadway *Williams'* as a possessive. This is a choice; one I make knowing it's not correct in the vein of the Classical *Zeus', Sophocles', Hercules', Jesus',* etc. . . . All of the recent openings of Williams' plays on Broadway have included the lonesome apostrophe, and to my thinking, if it's good enough for Broadway, it's good enough for me.

TENNESSEE
WILLIAMS
101

I

HOW TO GET TO TENNESSEE

Points of Interest

- Tennessee Williams was born Thomas Lanier Williams III.
- He was born on March 26, 1911, in Columbus, Mississippi.
- His family lived in the rectory of St. Paul's Episcopal Church and included:
    - his mother, Edwina;
    - his maternal grandmother, Rosina "Grand" Otte Dakin;
    - his maternal grandfather, Rev. Walter Dakin;
    - his sister, Rose;
    - and their domestic caretaker, Ozzie.
- His father, Cornelius "C. C." Coffin Williams, was a traveling salesman based in Knoxville and visited sporadically.
- After leaving Columbus in 1913, the family would move to Nashville, Tennessee, and Canton, Mississippi.
- In 1917, the Dakins and Williamses moved to Clarksdale, Mississippi. While in Clarksdale, Tom acquired diphtheria and nearly died.

- In 1918, Cornelius was promoted to a management position at his job, and the Williamses relocated to St. Louis.
- In 1919, Edwina and Cornelius had a third child, Dakin Williams.

When Thomas Lanier Williams III was born in Columbus, Mississippi, in a hospital building that's now a bank, he was taken home to a house that still stands thanks to the grace and planning of some pragmatic, literary-minded residents of the charming town. To save the Victorian from demolition, it needed to be moved from where it originally stood. It was resettled into a prominent spot right on the main drag of downtown. If you visit the historic home now, it's a welcome center for the hamlet, which was once known as Possum Town. Inside, you can find some of the Williamses' and Dakins' original furniture next to some period-appropriate stand-ins. Upstairs there's a timeline of Tennessee Williams' life and downstairs is a downright precious gift shop bursting at the seams. When I visited, a document in the upstairs hall immediately snagged my attention.

Hanging in a frame you can see the D.A.R. registration of Mrs. Edwina Dakin Williams, mother of America's greatest playwright. The Daughters of the American Revolution is a ladies' social and historical group to which the writer's mother belonged. A few of its dotted lines remain empty, but the registration still bears all the necessary signatures to validate it. It's dated November 8, 1911—only a few months after her first son was born. She was a busy lady by 1911 standards: children *and* a social calendar to tend to!

Curiously, the field labeled "Wife of" remains blank although her application bears her married name, Williams. Even so, she did *indeed* possess a husband. Cornelius Coffin Williams married young Edwina, a transplant from Ohio, and together they had a daughter named Rose and then a son named Tom. In the early years of their marriage, they resided together, but once Rose was in the picture, Edwina opted to stay in the home of her father, the Reverend Walter Edwin Dakin. Reverend Dakin was the preacher at St. Paul's Episcopal Church. His wife, Rosina Otte Dakin, helped her daughter to raise the children. A hired servant named Ozzie completed the household. She managed the kids and fostered Tom's robust imagination and penchant for clever turns of phrase. Eventually Ozzie set off on a trip to visit family, from which she never returned. She left behind in Tom an activated imagination and robust vocabulary.

While Reverend Dakin kept busy at the church and the women were busy with the housekeeping and child-wrangling, Cornelius spent much of his time on the road. He was a traveling salesman peddling men's clothing and later, shoes. When not on the road, Cornelius made a home in Knoxville, Tennessee—his home state. His absence suited Edwina and company just fine. Cornelius had seemed to be a disarming gentleman, but upon closer inspection in the wedded arena, it turned out that he and Edwina could not have been less ideal a match. They fought anytime he was near. His tumultuous arrival generally heralded unstable, violent episodes.

Predictably, the children grew to prefer time away from Cornelius. In fairness, the children's apprehension toward Cornelius might have had several contributing factors, such as his absence making him an outsider and the kids' being under the care of mostly women and the gregarious and mild Reverend—unlike Cornelius in every way.

Williams later intimated in his writing that his father called him "Miss Nancy" and treated him in other hurtful ways for what Cornelius perceived to be unmanly deportment. Cornelius was similarly standoffish to Rose, and as she grew older, they only understood one another less. Whatever the particulars of father's detachment, the Williams children were fortunate to have a nurturing homelife with the Dakins.

After several years in Columbus, the Dakins relocated to other parishes including ones in Nashville, Tennessee, and Canton, Mississippi. The Williamses followed in tow. After Canton, the Dakin tribe put down roots in Clarksdale, Mississippi, the heart of the Mississippi Delta region. It's at this juncture that I feel compelled to veer off on a momentary **detour** and explain the Delta region. I am myself a product of the Mississippi Delta—specifically, Greenville. While Williams and I were born generations apart, I feel that we share much of the Delta experience based on what I recognize in his writing.

For readers unfamiliar with the Delta, the region includes the space between the Mississippi River and the hillier middle of the state, and stretches down from Memphis to about Vicksburg. It is *not,* as its name would suggest, a delta. Rather, it's a floodplain formed betwixt the Mississippi and Yazoo rivers. To locate the topographical/geographical delta of the Mississippi River, one must look further south, closer to New Orleans . . . but you didn't come here for a lesson on topography *or* geography, even if I am labeling detours and points of interest. Semantic digression aside, there's a lot to unpack when it comes to the capital-*D* Delta as a cultural space.

Characteristically, the Delta is flat. With relatively few trees, it is easy to peer out to one's limit of vision across miles of flat farmland with only a sparse dotting of foliage in the distance. The result is that the Delta sky seems limitless. Sparse as the trees are the still-tiny towns that dot the map. Each far-off settlement is a kingdom unto itself with its particular culture, politics, and tightly held secrets. The places relish their connection as fellow Delta locales, but are decidedly insular. Based on stories of the Delta elders and the writings of Williams, these statements were just as true in pre-War Clarksdale as they are today.

The distance between places and their curious, monolithic cultures present opportunities for mystery, suspense, and even comedy in their oral and written tradition. For example, Clarksdale is the site of the Crossroads of Blues—both a musical landmark and the setting for an allegory about a Faustian bargain for musical mastery. It's stories like those that make the Delta fertile ground for mythologizing and poeticizing the American South. That's just what Tennessee Williams would become famous for. The limitless sky became the vaulting ceiling in his Southern Gothic cathedral of imagination. His writing would become populated with composites of the various characters and locales he encountered in his Delta years. Delta details coalesced to make such mythic localities as Glorious Hill, Laurel, Blue Mountain, Two Rivers and Tiger Tail counties, and others. There'll be a more comprehensive detour on composites later, but **let's conclude this Delta detour** here.

In Clarksdale, Williams came down with a nasty case of diphtheria. For readers unfamiliar, as many will be nowadays (thank you, vaccines), the disease affects the nose and throat. It forms a thick, nasty mass at the back of the throat and can be quite serious. Tom's case was one of these serious cases. His road to recovery was long and left him too weak to engage in typical youthful antics. The skirmish with the Reaper left Tom forever fixated on death, illness, and the risk of suffocation. This fixation would surface regularly throughout his intimate and public life—more on this and other obsessions as we dive deeper; the wages of this and other traumas having clear and lasting effects on his body of work.

Williams lived in Clarksdale from 1917 to 1918, but spent many summers there after relocating to St. Louis. You may notice I said that the Dakins put roots down in Clarksdale. The Williamses were not so fortunate. In 1918, the rooster finally came home to . . . roost, I guess. The cock in question was Cornelius, and the roost he would come home to wasn't in Clarksdale. After several years on the road (and out of Edwina's hair), the shoe company promoted him to a manager, and with the promotion came a more regular lodging situation. He was relocated permanently to St. Louis, Missouri, and he brought the family with him—minus the grandparents, who had been pillars of young Tom's security.

From the idyllic, beautiful Delta where Tom had only just started schooling in earnest (only to be hobbled by diphtheria from which he was probably still recovering), the boy was snatched and dropped into smoggy, crowded St. Louis. He and his sister would be ostracized for their countrified behaviors and rustic accents. They no longer knew their place in the world, since being the preacher's grandchildren had always been a touchstone for them, socially. Then, there were the fights. With Cornelius and Edwina under the same roof in an ongoing way, so too were the fights ongoing. Gone were the roomy-enough rooms of the rectories the children had inhabited when living with the Dakins.

The children were sentenced to serve out their youth in cramped chambers in a hive-like apartment building. To a sensitive young man like Tom, this was absolute upheaval. He dubbed the town "The City of St. Pollution," and was determined to hate it.

It's worth mentioning, also, that Clarksdale was a boomtown during these years. The health of its agricultural economy was at its apex—a marked difference from today, where much of the South—and the Delta most of all—has suffered a nigh-debilitating economic downturn. In contrast, St. Louis seemed to have little to offer Tom. The un-scrapable skies populated with clouds for giants and the soil rich with creative minerals were replaced with smog, steel, and concrete. He was soft; St. Louis was hard. Tom would retreat to his grandparents' home for the summer for the remainder of his youth, even going so far as to spend the entire 1920-21 school year there.

Tom's frustration with his new, alien life in the industrial badlands of urban Missouri was aggravated by the most innocent of arrivals. Edwina and Cornelius had their third child shortly after arriving in St. Louis. They named him Dakin after Edwina's family (this is narratively confusing at times, I'll admit—Dakin is the brother, the Dakins are the grandparents, and *Reverend* Dakin is the grandfather. What's in a name?). Dakin was like a do-over for Cornelius: a chance at having a son who admired him and who wasn't effeminate like Tom. This drove the wedge deeper between Cornelius, Tom, and Rose.

Nevertheless, like sand in an oyster, St. Louis would be the irritant to produce some of Williams' jewels. To escape the misery of his new unhappy life, he employed a few strategies. First, he spent copious time with his sister, growing ever closer to her. Second, he would visit his grandparents in Clarksdale any chance he got. He'd go on visits to sick and troubled parishioners with his grandfather and entertain visiting townspeople with his grandmother in the rectory's parlor. These visits instilled in him a bestiary of Southern creatures that he would later unleash in his famous plays, but his writing had to start somewhere. Another pastime Tom enjoyed in his youth was writing. His early childhood scribbles in crayon and lead did not escape Edwina's notice. She decided to encourage his writing and bought him a secondhand Underwood portable typewriter. From that moment in 1924, practically no day passed that Williams didn't lay his hands on a typewriter.

Ironically for a writer who would become known for the autobiographical nature of his characters and situations, young Tom wrote seemingly from abject inexperience with his topics. The first of his essays to ever be published was an answer to the question "Can a good wife be a good sport?" in *Smart Set* magazine. In his entry to the amateur writing contest, he would posit that: No, in fact, a good sport could never make a good wife, since a good sport was, to young Tom, synonymous with an adulteress. He went so far as to share an anecdote about coming home to his own good sport of a wife engaged in flagrant infidelity. The year was 1927. Tom had never been married. Tom was sixteen years old. Tom had pulled the story from whence the sun had never shone.

In 1928, Tom was published a second time. The vehicle for his imaginings this time was a magazine called *Weird Tales.* The periodical was famous for publishing fantasy, horror, and early science fiction. Williams' offering to the magazine was a short story called "The Vengeance of Nitocris," in which an Egyptian queen avenges her brother's murder by luring his assailants into the bottom of a pyramid for a dinner party, whereupon she seals them in the chamber and floods it, drowning them. Because, again, you write what you know—no, of course, Tom had once again produced a story purely from his fantastical musings (read: his butt). Regardless of their origins, the stories were being put into print. Along with a few amateur local poetry accolades, Tom was building some confidence and a résumé as a budding writer.

Between his discipline for writing regularly and his various small stepping stones to success, he was able to realistically dream of a future as a working writer through high school. When he graduated, he went on to pursue a journalism degree at University of Missouri at Columbia. Not too far from St. Louis, Columbia allowed Tom to spread his wings creatively and intellectually. It was in Columbia that he began to explore his sexuality, too. He explored crushes—mostly unrequited—for both men and women in his time at the university. Of only a few substantial and substantiated instances of his interest in a member of the opposite sex, one was at Mizzou. To hear him (or read of him) recounting it, it was more of an awkward farce than a love for the ages as some have tried to imagine it. Before university, he had professed love for a young woman named Hazel Kramer, but while sincere, was neither sexual nor long-lived.

Also significant about his time at Mizzou, Tom wrote his first one-act play. It was called *Beauty Is the Word,* and it placed sixth in the Drama Arts Club play contest. While it didn't receive one of the top prizes and neither was it performed, it was Tom's first step toward writing for the stage.

Tom spent much of his time at university

exploring his own writing style and socializing, putting forth perfunctory effort in his studies. His studies, it would seem, bored him. One in particular, Reserve Officer Training Corps, would be his undoing at Mizzou. When Tom flunked ROTC in 1931, Cornelius seized the opportunity to pull his sissy-boy son out of school and put him to honest work. I can't imagine that having another family member at home, working during the Depression didn't account for some part of Corneilus's machinations, but neither can I point to any solid evidence for that theory. Whatever his reasons for doing so, Cornelius earned no love from Tom when he pulled him back to another round of torture in the concrete vise of St. Pollution.

Returning home would be worse than Tom could fathom. Not only was he yanked back into the tumultuous back-and-forth between Ma and Pa, but Rose's mental health showed signs of deteriorating. Tom, sensitive as he was, couldn't help but observe the changes in her. He was pitifully ill-equipped to help her as she blossomed as an emotionally complex adult in a home that valued a prim, demure, and obedient woman. And, of course, there was young Dakin, a walking, talking, reminder of Cornelius's preference against Tom (through no fault of Dakin, who was not yet a teen!).

Compounding the stress of the homestead, Tom had to earn a wage for the first time in his life. Cornelius secured him a job at the shoe warehouse. Tom hated the shoe warehouse—one of many blazingly autobiographical fragments that compose *The Glass Menagerie*. Tom grimaced and bore the pangs of the adjustment, going so far as to ride to work with his father doing whatever the passenger version of white-knuckling the whole trip is. They would say little to one another, suspended on these commutes to the shoe factory in a respectful, painful silence. As a veteran writer and shaman of the human spirit, Tennessee Williams would look back at these rides and so many other interactions with Cornelius with forgiveness and even tenderness, finally realizing that it was their incompatibility and incomprehension of each other that caused this pain, and not some purposeful slight. Regardless, Williams would use this and manifold other reasons to hate Cornelius through the 1930s and into the 1940s.

Let's take another quick **detour** here. By now, we have tiptoed around mentions of composites, archetypes, and autobiographical details filtering into Willams' writing. Let's begin shaping that point early. It is widely known that Williams would mutate his experience at the shoe factory and in St. Louis generally into a handful of plays and short stories exploring claustrophobic living circumstances—both in the sense of "living with" people and just "living" writ large.

The most notable example of a "St. Louis Play" is *The Glass Menagerie.* The tale of an aspiring writer who lives in a cramped St. Louis apartment while being driven slowly batty by his overbearing mother and his job at a shoe factory. Williams goes so far as to name the character Tom Wingfield (abbreviated T. W.). Tom the character is held in his cage primarily by duty to his sister, a shy and socially inadequate young woman with grim future prospects. Writing was Tom's pressure release valve in the St. Louis period, to be sure . . . and the world may never know how closely some of his fictional details relate to reality.

Menagerie is now recognized as a quintessential Mid-Century American drama, but at the time of its first production, it was anything but quintessential. It focused on a struggling family and its secrets, sure, but it wasn't—as was often the case—about the trials and tribulations of folks who had made it hitting stumbling blocks. *Menagerie,* like other plays being developed and presented at the time, was about folks who had never quite "made it" coping with the exigencies of their unfulfilled circumstances.

More literally, *Menagerie* is about a family—the Wingfields—who live in a crummy flat in a hive-like building in St. Louis. The son works at a shoe factory, the mother, Amanda, struggles to make ends meet for her children, and the sister, Laura, is debilitated by shyness and a physical handicap that is never named but has compounded her emotional and social nervousness. The father is absent, having left several years ago. These characters were all sculpted out of bits of material that Williams curated in his lifetime, but they were pieced together to make characters to forward the plot—not to share the author's life story.

Writing was therapeutic and helped Tom to release some of the rancor for family and work, but it must be stated at this early point in the retrospective that Tennessee Williams the writer was not Tom Wingfield the character—nor wholly any character he wrote. Williams was a master at building *composites* from live specimens, himself included. Moving among Tennessee Williams circles, one of the most common headaches I receive is the one associated with someone who tries to too closely relate Williams to his characters. There's no denying Williams was a shamelessly autobiographical writer. However, he wrote plays, poems, and stories about *characters,* all of whom he gave unique lives and drew from several fonts of inspiration. That's all to say, his characters are more complex than just being portraits of real people.

One needs only to look so far as the names of the characters in *The Glass Menagerie* for evidence of this: Amanda and Laura Wingfield were never meant to be some great tributes to the monoliths of Edwina and Rose Williams, respectively. When Williams wrote them, there was no great cultural understanding of his own concern with his mother and sister. Laura and Amanda had to be recognizable and relatable portraits before the Tennessee-Williams-as-famous-writer paradigm. Certainly, there were several bits of Williams himself in Tom Wingfield, and Jim O'Connor (the Gentleman Caller) was even the name of a chum of his from the Missouri days, but even they were composites constructed of both dramatic elements, needs of the play, and details from the playwright's life.

Delving more deeply, Laura's afflictions look nothing like Rose's looked. Rose had no physical malady and shyness was not exactly her issue. Amanda claims a Southern upbringing, but Edwina was from Ohio—no matter how brazenly she wore her badge of Southernity (I'm sure I didn't make that word up, but if I did, you can use it). Most notably, the father in *Menagerie* is absent: exactly the opposite of Cornelius in the Missouri period. Plus, there's no Dakin character. As you'll learn in future pages, Tom Williams didn't up and leave, skipping the light fantastic and leaving the family high and dry like Tom Wingfield, and the Williamses never suffered the same poverty as the Wingfields. And so ends the **detour.**

Points of Interest

- In 1924 in St. Louis, Edwina buys Tom a second-hand Underwood Portable typewriter.
- In 1927, Tom publishes in *Smart Set* for his essay answer to the prompt "Can a Good Wife Be a Good Sport?"
- In 1928, Tom is published a second time. His story "The Vengeance of Nitocris" is set down in *Weird Tales* magazine.
- Tom seeks a journalism degree from the University of Missouri at Columbia (Mizzou) in 1929.
- In 1930, Tom's first one-act play entitled *Beauty Is the Word* places in a university contest. It is not staged.
- In 1932, Tom is taken out of college by his father for flunking ROTC and put to work at the International Shoe Company.

Much like Tom Wingfield, Tom Williams was not cut out for warehouse life. In 1935, Tom collapsed from exhaustion, seemingly a combination of a nervous breakdown and a plethora of habits unbecoming a working man such as late-night poetry binges and seldom sleeping. Jobless and awash in uncertainty, Tom was sent to Memphis, where the Dakins now resided, to recuperate over the summer. This summer, I argue, is one of the most significant in a series of significant summers in Tom Williams' life.

THE SCENIC ROUTE

Other St. Louis plays and stories of note include *Stairs to the Roof,* a fantasy about the workers in dead-end jobs and how they can escape in the most miraculous and bizarre ways. It's a fascinating read from a young playwright because of science-fictional overtones and elements that echo Bertolt Brecht and even *Machinal* by Sophie

Treadwell and *The Adding Machine* by Elmer Rice (there was a concern in the day of machines taking over human work and humankind. *Hm.*). To be back under Edwina's roof, Tom's personal, romantic, and sexual development were frequently put on pause—his mother's puritanical hovering casting scrutiny on any type of "heathen" activity. It's likely that Tom operated in secret, the embers of his sexuality not being quite extinguished yet—in fact, perhaps burning more ferociously under the surface. He would later juxtapose day-to-day doldrums with extreme sensuality in stories like "Desire and the Black Masseur."

II

SOUTH AS THE RIVER FLOWS

Points of Interest

- While recuperating in Memphis from a nervous breakdown, Tom co-authors *Cairo! Shanghai! Bombay!* with Bernice Dorothy Shapiro, his next-door neighbor. The play is performed that summer by a group called the Garden Players.
- Also in 1935, Tom audits in Washington University in St. Louis. He formally enrolls in January 1936.
- The same year, Tom sees Russian actress Alla Nazimova star in Henrik Ibsen's *Ghosts,* which made lasting impressions on his style—particularly his focus on complex women characters.
- In 1936-37, local and university groups produce some of Williams' plays including *The Magic Tower, Candles to the Sun,* and *Fugitive Kind.*
- In 1937, Tom transfers to the University of Iowa to formally study playwriting. Meanwhile, Rose is committed to an institution for mental problems.
- In 1938, freshly graduated from Iowa, Tom submits his plays under a pseudonym and some false pretenses on his way to New Orleans.

The summer in Memphis with the Dakins provided respite from warehouse work, but it did not alleviate Tom's duty to his craft—no, not shoe factory clerking, his other craft. Ever the compulsive author, he continued working on poetry, prose, and most notably plays in his convalescence. A neighbor girl, Bernice Dorothy Shapiro, headed a troupe of amateur theatre artists named the Garden Players (because they played in—you guessed it—a garden). She invited Tom to collaborate with her on that summer's offering. What would come of their imaginations' churning was a melodrama called *Cairo! Shanghai! Bombay!* about some sailors on shore leave and hunting for some loose women . . . because, again, you write what you (don't) know. Shapiro took top billing as author although she wrote only the prologue and epilogue. It was produced by her group of local thespians, after all.

Cairo! Shanghai! Bombay! wasn't reviewed by any national critics to be sure, but it still had significance: it was the first time Tom's work was performed in front of an audience (albeit the performers were local amateurs, and the audience was likely captive relatives and other well-wishers). This was a catalyzing moment because it showed Tom, who before this point had only been praised with sixth place in a university contest for *Beauty Is the Word,* that there were much more valuable prizes for his creative output: applause and laughter—and later their moody big sister, catharsis.

Tom spent a good deal of time that summer in a nearby library, too, where he ate up as much inspiration as he could. It was there that he was first captivated by the writings of Russian dramatist Anton Chekhov, becoming acquainted with his personal and probing style of characterization.

From the library aisles, Williams exercised his imagination and his ravenous desire to be a citizen of a wild and diverse planet.

Feeling energized and spiritually restored (or something like), Tom returned to St. Louis in the fall. He audited classes at Washington University and was admitted in January of 1936. Wash U seemed a more stable situation at least financially, since it was in the city and Tom was able to live at home. A pair of literary-minded friends helped to assuage any household conflict. Two fellow students, Clark Mills McBurney and William Jay Smith would congregate with Tom and read over, revise, and reflect on their own work as well as the writings of their favorite poets and authors. Tom learned that his craft was bolstered when he was surrounded by others with his passion and whose writing he admired.

He continued writing and attending plays during his Wash U days from 1935 to 1937. He witnessed Alla Nazimova in a touring production of Henrik Ibsen's *Ghosts* staged by the Theatre Guild. They'll come up again, so don't forget the Theatre Guild. Another noteworthy Russian occupied his attention during this period, too. The playwright Anton Chekhov became his aesthetic north star for a period, seasoned with the sensibilities of writers like the not-long-dead Hart Crane, D. H. Lawrence, Rainer Maria Rilke, and dramatists Ibsen and Eugene O'Neill.

Mini-Detour: If we don't agree that Williams was America's greatest playwright (fine—subjective; whatever), we can at least agree that for a time he was America's foremost playwright. What makes the writer himself foremost American, I would argue, is that his style and sensibilities are an intricate latticework of influences from global and domestic writers. As voraciously as Williams wrote, consuming blank pages and turning out word-pocked ones, he also absorbed tricks, techniques, and themes that struck him. From the French Arthur Rimbaud to the Japanese Yukio Mishima, he never solidified his style so much that it could not be metamorphosed into something more diverse and closer to truth. That, and not apple pie, is what makes him foremost American as a playwright, and what set him up to be America's foremost playwright. **End detour.**

After *Cairo! Shanghai! Bombay!,* Tom could not be satisfied to take sixth place in academic playwriting contests. He needed to see his plays staged. Luckily for him, there were local groups chomping at the bit for new plays, particularly ones that showed the struggles and victories of the downtrodden (read: plays with socialist leanings). The first such group was the suburban Theatre Guild of Webster Groves, who produced *The Magic Tower,* about an unhappy couple tempted by a life apart from their circumstances. In the spring of 1937, Tom's first full-length play was put on by a St. Louis-based theatre group called the Mummers. It was titled *Candles to the Sun* and featured the plight of a mining town being destroyed by its boss's greed. Its hero's name was Red. Red, like socialism. The boss is suggested to represent capitalist greed.

The Mummers also staged *Fugitive Kind,* another full-length play. By November, when it was staged, Tom had already transferred to the University of Iowa to study playwriting formally. The university was and still is known for its strong writing programs. Tom only spent a year at Iowa, but it was a valuable year for his craft. Unfortunately, in the space of time in which Tom was absent, the family came to the conclusion that Rose's behavior needed amending—decisively and forcibly.

Rose was long-fraught with behavior labeled as disturbed and disturbing. Suffice to say that Rose was stifled and acting out. Rose had a terrible time coming of age. Edwina obviously favored Tom; C. C., Dakin—both parents bordering on contempt for Rose. She had a handful of disastrous relationships, a failed debut when she was sent up for finishing school in Knoxville, and one of her romantic prospects even died. Her mental health's decline was incremental, and although her troubles weren't invisible to Tom, he lacked the tools to do much about it.

Some of Rose's acting out came in the form of language and suggestions that Edwina considered sexually vulgar. It is here that Edwina's eccentric puritanical streak became insidious. Unable to cope with her unfit-for-polite-society daughter, Edwina sought a diagnosis for her precious, disturbed child. The diagnosis was dementia praecox (the term was a precursor for a diagnosis now more likely to have been schizophrenia). Faced with such a dire pronouncement, Edwina became convinced that extreme treatments were necessary. The first such treatment was to commit Rose to a Catholic convalescent home (i.e., a torture camp with nuns for overlords. And to this day, I cannot figure why this isn't the setting of a Tennessee Williams play.). Next, she was moved to a state hospital and given shock treatments. For those who have been fortunate enough to live exclusively in a world where some such treatments have been banished to obscurity: medical professionals put instruments on the young woman's temples and zapped her to make her stop talking about nasty subjects in front of company.

Tom was justifiably upset by these things when he learned about them. He was forced to balance his own dreams against the responsibility he felt to protect his sister, who had been sometimes his protector. He pressed on developing his craft as a writer and living his life as a young man at university . . . even if he was becoming long in the tooth for that lifestyle, he reckoned. At Iowa, he encountered Professor Mabie, a writing scholar who gave him such a devastating dressing down of his long play *Spring Storm* that Tom tucked away the manuscript never to be shared again, explaining why it wasn't until after his death that it ever saw a performance! A nasty teacher's critique can exact a dire toll on a young artist, but Tom was undaunted. *Spring Storm* reflected coming of age in the Delta and has curiously autobiographical overtures. Might Mabie have soured Tom's taste for autobiographical drama for a time? Maybe.

Mabie be damned, in summer of 1938, he finally obtained his college degree. Tom Williams graduated from the University of Iowa with a bachelor's degree in August at age 27—an age that proved a challenge for his next adventure.

Tom had to figure out what to do next. He'd been in school or longing to be in school his entire life until this point, and he found himself in St. Louis with a degree in writing and no obvious prospects. He knew he needed to keep churning out work and that St. Louis was no place to do it. He set his sights on the Works Progress Administration's Federal Writers' Project. The WPA was a New Deal agency whose goal was to put job seekers to work following the widespread unemployment of the Great Depression. Most biographies and narratives about Williams' life sidestep or overlook the cultural impact of the Great Depression. Based on Williams' correspondence and journals at the time, he didn't seem expressly impacted, but it is noteworthy to observe that the financial crisis and the space of time it took for the nation to rebound was a part of the overall climate in which Williams came up. At any rate, the FWP was a branch of the greater agency and had an office in a place that was of distinct interest to Williams: New Orleans.

Considered a capital-B Bohemian Capitol, New Orleans had everything Williams was interested in: a vibrant arts scene, a low cost of living, inspiring vistas for people-watching, a WPA branch to employ him, and what he expected was a safe haven from his family's puritanical influences. Once Tom had begun to sow his wild oats, they couldn't be cast back into the field. Our hero was beginning to express physical desire that had been long repressed in the shadows of churches and Edwina herself. New Orleans was a place where he could explore his sexuality unchecked.

Whether or not Edwina's ultimate nightmare would become manifest, and Tom would be cursed to devolve into an insatiable sexual degenerate down the line was immaterial—it would remain her fear no matter how well Tom did. Regardless of his vices, Tom was never one to neglect his work. On his way down from St. Louis to New Orleans, he submitted his plays for consideration in a writing contest held by the Group Theatre. The problem, as I mentioned, came in the criteria for the *young* writers hoping to submit. They needed to be *young: younger* than Tom. Thus beginning his tense relationship with age-related stories, Williams fudged his age on the application, claiming 1914 to be his birth year, making himself three years younger and thus meeting the 25-years-or-younger requirement. To ensure nobody caught onto his conceit, he dropped the plays in the mail from his grandparents' home in Memphis and used a pseudonym: Tennessee Williams.

Detour: According to the account in his own *Memoirs,* Williams took on the moniker "Tennessee" as an homage to his frontier forefathers, the Laniers. One of his ancestors, Sidney Lanier, was a poet of great acclaim, a point of pride for Williams. Williams began using the pseudonym in that Iowa-toward-New Orleans period. For all the conjecture, this is the story of Tennessee Williams as Tom Williams' name. That's it. There are accounts, tenuously substantiated, that suggest it was a nickname he got in college because of his southern drawl; his classmates were unable to remember Mississippi or something. There are suggestions that he just came up with it when dropping the manuscripts in the mail because he was in Memphis, *Tennessee.* There are several stories as to the first utterance of the name. Sadly, anyone with direct knowledge of that moment is dead, and we can't know for sure. So here we are, with a writer who chose to submit plays to a professional group under the nom de plume that he'd continue using for the rest of his life. I'll leave it at that and let the folks with the time machine sort it out . . . but to hear him tell it, it's the Laniers story. **End detour.**

With his plays dropped in the mail under a new name with a fake age and a far-flung address, Tennessee-né-Thomas Williams was free to fling himself into the decadent, catch-as-catch-can writer's life in New Orleans—a sinking city at the end of the world full of danger, grit, and glory for those who could plunder it without themselves being plundered. He lighted in a rooming house on his first night in the city and was immediately inducted into the party culture of the city in the winter of late 1938. Within a few days, he had hopped to the famed rooming house at 722 Toulouse Street, the setting for his 1977 play

Vieux Carré. There he met the cast of real-life characters whose souls he would burn into words while transfiguring their bodies and features with a pallet of composite traits in a multitude of plays.

In *Vieux Carré,* Williams puts the phrase "Writers are shameless spies." in the mouth of his character The Writer (another character with T. W. initials). That's just what Williams was doing: spying on life and distilling the truth of situations into pure form in his dramas, poems, and stories. It's a shame he didn't get a job at the WPA the whole time he was in New Orleans, especially since its office was just down the block from his Toulouse Street room. Employed or not, it was a valuable period for Tennessee as a writer.

Tom left the city just after Mardi Gras in 1939 (that's late winter or early spring, depending on Easter, for y'all outside-of-New-Orleans folk). Before he did, he memorized the faces and features of the French Quarter characters like his landlady Mrs. Anderson, whom he transformed into Mrs. Wire the landlady in *Vieux Carré.* He spent his time in the city awash in the vibrant, mad parade—but it was a single individual that washed him out of the city.

THE SCENIC ROUTE

Mrs. Wire was not the only French Quarter character Williams drew composites from in his many years visiting and living in New Orleans. Ranging from close friends to acquaintances, they echo in dozens of his plays, stories, and poems. The hustlers, the barkers, and the lost featured in his short story "One Arm" and his poem "Mornings on Bourbon Street" are fascinating examples. These ephemeral figures would leave impressions that he kept with him forty years into the future, long after they faded from sight and contact. The off-beat and cast-off wanderers of New Orleans fit nicely into Williams' caste of the Fugitive Kind, which is explored throughout this book.

New Orleans was a nexus of class and race, which did not escape Williams' notice. New Orleans-based plays such as *Vieux Carré, A Streetcar Named Desire, Green Eyes, Lord Byron's Love Letter, Mr. Paradise, The Lady of Larkspur Lotion, Auto-Da-Fé, Suddenly Last Summer,* and others delve into these politics while also illustrating the tenderness that exists in the underbelly of the Crescent City.

III

At the "Tennessee" Line

Points of Interest

- In 1939, Tennessee Williams, as he is now calling himself, lives for a short time in New Orleans before setting off with runaway school teacher Jim Parrot to parts west, ultimately landing in Southern California.
- In 1939, Williams wins a "special prize" from the Group Theatre for his submission in their play contest.
- Also in 1939, Williams meets Audrey Wood. She would be his literary agent for many years.
- In 1940, Williams relocates to New York and studies playwriting at The New School. He is also commissioned to write a play for the Theatre Guild.

Jim Parrot was a musician and school teacher from Florida who, like Tennessee, sought momentary refuge in New Orleans. For Parrot, the Crescent City was temporary. His sights were set farther West. Finding little in the way of paying prospects for writing in New Orleans, Tennessee saw no reason to remain.

The thought of adventuring out West with a daring stranger struck him, and so he went—Williams was attracted to the lure of transience, both in his life and his writing. The topic of transience would work its way into several of his themes, often juxtaposed against circumstances of feeling stuck in place.

The end of Williams and Parrot's excursion was California, but along the way they shared many unusual exploits. They siphoned gas with their mouths to fuel their journey. After stealing fuel, they were even so bold as to drop in on Frieda Lawrence, widow of D. H. Lawrence, whom Williams greatly admired. Mrs. Lawrence held court amid a cabal of lady writer friends, who were charming to Williams. Williams and Parrot spent nights under a sky as expansive as the Delta listening to coyotes bay in the distance. What the boys did not spend a lot of time doing was checking the mail. If they had, Tennessee might have been easier to track, for one individual was in hot pursuit, unbeknownst to our hero.

Back East, Molly Day Thacher was in the employ of the Group Theatre. She had been involved in the selection of the winners of the contest for young writers—remember the plays Williams had dumped in the mail in Memphis? Thacher decided the plays of the "twenty-five"-year-old unknown Tennessee Williams didn't achieve first, second, or third place in the contest. However, the writing did deserve some sort of recognition. The plays received what was dubbed a "special prize" from the Group Theatre and had an award of $100 attached—leaving Molly Thacher with the onerous task of finding the author during his westward adventure.

It was no easy feat, but eventually Thacher tracked Williams down in August of 1939. Williams was elated to have won, and that's not all. The exposure from winning the contest piqued the curiosity of another savvy New York lady, who summoned him from Laguna Beach across the continent. The $100 prize from the Group Theatre was nice, but it's the fateful connection made in Manhattan that would be one of the most significant in his lifetime.

Excited but bewildered, Tennessee arrived at the offices of Liebling-Wood Agency in a tattered sweater. He was awash in a sea of chorus girls who were hoping to book work through Bill Liebling. At the end of the day, when Tennessee was told there was nothing in the way of acting roles for men that day, he corrected the situation by indicating he was there to see Wood, *not* Liebling. Wood was a literary agent, her husband was the talent agent!

Audrey Wood was a sharp, formidable representative whose attention to detail was a perfect complement to Tennessee's penchant for seat-of-the-pants-style living. He was capturing squabs on a ranch in Southern California when Thacher beckoned him, after all. They're young pigeons for eating, if you were wondering. Now it was Audrey Wood's turn to take a baby bird under her wing and guide him to literary fame—or at least fiscal sustainability through writing. Unknowingly, she was joining a coven of women that would continue to build the scaffolding for Williams' career.

The next year was a busy period of training and growth for Williams. Shortly after gaining representation, Williams was published in *Story* magazine. The short story "The Field of Blue Children" was the first time the adopted name Tennessee Williams appeared in print. Once he garnered recognition for being in publication, Audrey snagged Williams a $1,000 grant from the Rockefeller Foundation. Williams still needed to work on his craft for drama, it was decided, and he enrolled in early 1940 at The New School, where he studied under Erwin Piscator and John Gassner. His classmates and colleagues included Arthur

Miller, Clifford Odets, and William Saroyan. At this time he was learning his skills as a theatre-maker while also being swept up into a literary scene more robust than he could have been prepared for by any auxiliary club in St. Louis or garden troupe in Memphis. Come the summer of 1940, he booked a gig. Now equipped with a more critical eye and connections to the great writers of the time, Tennessee was charged with constructing a play for the Theatre Guild (yes, that one; told you they'd come back up).

The harried and hedonistic New York scene Williams had been gobbling up had also been gobbling on him. This presented a challenge, creatively. His concentration was regularly interrupted by the hustle and bustle of opportunities to socialize, explore the city, and . . . well, to get swept up in all of the things that make New York, New York, a hell of a town. When the city that never sleeps exhausted Williams, he decided to relocate somewhere more serene while he went through drafts and revisions of his creative labor. The perfect spot presented itself in the locale of Provincetown, Massachusetts, on Cape Cod. Several factors made it perfect for Tennessee to craft a masterpiece. Foremost, it was not abuzz with the jumble of infinite diversions like New York City. Next, it was situated a short ferry ride away from Boston, where the play he was working on would ultimately have its out-of-town tryout. Out-of-town tryouts in theatre are when shows have performances in another market before moving to a larger one—for example, Williams' *Battle of Angels* tried out in Boston in hopes of garnering a Broadway run in New York City. It's a common practice for shows to work out their kinks before moving to more expensive venues.

The other reasons Williams was drawn to the

Cape more or less echoed the list of New Orleans's finer points: it was a Bohemian oasis amid a puritanical region; it provided enough business to feel alive while presenting opportunities for retreating to complete artistic duties; and it was full of gay men, lesbians, queer folk, and every other type of sexually marginalized people.

A detour, to unpack: I think it's time for the birds and the bees talk—that is, the Tennessee Williams' sexuality talk. Perhaps it's **not a detour** so much as a **swerve.** Williams was gay, end stop. In recent years, it has become less shocking for folks to cope with the notion that America's greatest playwright was an unabashedly gay man. During his lifetime it was often a point of contention for other people—not so much for him. There have even been those who have tried to ascribe the label of bisexual to him postmortem because of descriptions of a fledgling romance with a young woman named Hazel Kramer while he was a pre-teen in St. Louis and an account of one sexual endeavor with a rapacious girl named Bette in Iowa in his vast compendium of writings, public and private. *This* writer equates that as a stretch at best and gay erasure at worst. Regardless of posthumous musings, however, there is a great body of evidence that Williams enjoyed, exalted, and eroticized men.

He suggested in his writings that there was some slap-and-tickle in his college years. Expression of his sexual urges became more overt and intense in New Orleans and Southern California. One of the most distracting diversions in New York was his proclivity for cruising public spots and camping with his "sisters"—other gay men in the literary sphere ("camp" is gay slang for over-the-top, outrageous tone, attitude, and expression, particularly using coded gay lingo, references, and gestures. It also refers to a style, which is exaggerated but controlled, and which features elements of the above attitude, expression, tone, etc.).

In Provincetown, Williams found more than just camaraderie and one-night stands. In the bohemian idyll, he found his first mature love. The object of Tennessee's affection was Kip Kiernan, a draft-dodging Canadian dancer who, like Tennessee, adopted a pseudonym. His given name was Bernard Dubowski. And here we find ourselves swerving back onto the main path, **ending our detour.**

Looking at Tennessee's writing, it can be inferred that Williams was much more invested in Kip than the dancer was in him. Kip had what appeared to be an affectionate tolerance for Tennessee, and even allowed some sexual liberty, but shortly after they parted ways, Kip married a woman and proceeded to have what seemed to be marital bliss until his untimely death by brain cancer only a few years later. Nevertheless, Tennessee was head-over-heels, butterflies-in-his-tummy gaga over Kip. When Kip wasn't rehearsing his dances and Tennessee wasn't writing or swimming, they spent hours together with other members of the artistic community carousing and conferring on topics of cultural significance (probably Communism, sexuality, and other grievous, occult subjects).

A summer went by and Tennessee turned out a play while eking out a meager Cape living on advances (the money publishers front to keep their contracted writers tided over until publication . . . if the writers are exceedingly lucky). After exhausting himself in P-Town, Williams took a few months off in Mexico to bask in the equatorial climes and rejuvenate before heading to Boston to see the fruits of his labor. While he was there, he took in more than just the hot, dense air. He drew from the scenery and personages. As he had with the characters and corners of New Orleans and St. Louis, he took mental notes to reference for his future inventions. The impressions that Mexico left him with carried through to his writings for decades. After refreshing himself and overcoming the gulf of empty space that Kip left unoccupied at summer's end, Williams headed back up north to see his play staged by the Theatre Guild.

Battle of Angels is a Southern tragedy set in a fictionalized Mississippi Delta town reminiscent of Clarksdale and other nearby boroughs. It concerns a town full of ladies whose loins are set atwitter when a young tramp comes into town and begins working for a prominent town scion's wife. It ends in murder and mayhem, and a blaze that engulfs the protagonists literally after the fire of desire had been set figuratively to the ladies' underthings. That synopsis does it very little justice for all its complexity. However, its complexity was perhaps a major contributing factor to its failure: it flopped in Boston.

The star power behind its famous leading lady, Miriam Hopkins, was not enough to secure a Broadway run for the doomed drama. Boston in the early 1940s was a Puritan stronghold, so all of the sexuality in the play ran afoul of censors and straitlaced theatregoers. To top it all off, the fire effect was not thoroughly vetted before the audience arrived. The attendees and cast were choked on smoke and spilled out of the theatre hacking and dismayed. Miriam Hopkins is said to have apologetically winced as she struggled through her curtain call. Audience, critics, and Theatre Guild were unforgiving of the whole affair. After the seemingly fortuitous arrangements made by Audrey Wood and the Theatre Guild, it was not Tennessee Williams' year.

Williams spiraled into a depression and, like the time he could not bear to work in the warehouse anymore, he needed to escape and recuperate. He traveled far and wide, writing all the way. In spite of his devastation at the failure of *Battle,* he was undaunted in his creative routine. He still woke every day and set to writing for hours wherever he was. The years 1941 and '42 were spent in all manner of homes, hotels, and hovels. He spent some time in St. Louis with the family. He visited his "sister" writers in New York. He popped around to various rooming houses, rented rooms, and guest rooms in New Orleans and Provincetown. He stayed with family of friends here and there in places like Nantucket Island and Macon, Georgia. He even dipped back south of the border into Mexico for a spell, having been so charmed with it. One imagines it to be an astonishing walkabout when considering the cost of travel as I write this, but that's inflation for you.

Perhaps the most curious detour was Williams' time in Jacksonville, Florida, when he worked for (*believe it or not!*) Uncle Sam at the office of the US Engineers. Regardless of leanings that conservatives would later deem un-American, Tennessee was staunchly anti-fascist. He detailed his disdain for Nazis in communications to a small number of friends, even going so far as to wish a boisterous, Nazi-sympathizing German tourist in Mexico be fatally bit by a scorpion (Williams did not understand scorpions use their stings to deliver venom, not by biting . . . He was less an expert on arachnids and more into the intricacies of the human condition). Williams liked the Jacksonville job pretty well because it allowed him to work late nights, write at his leisure, and enjoy coastal life. He could not serve the government in any more physically involved role, even as war cast its shadow across the whole world. Tennessee's eyes and heart were unfit for military service. Dakin, on the other hand, was called to serve. While the world warred, Tennessee wrote, among the others fortunate enough to be spared the battlefield.

In 1942, his circulation in variegated writing circles paid off in a substantial way. He was introduced to James Laughlin, a steelmaking legacy who had no flair for metal. Instead, Laughlin, who Tennessee would come to call "Jay" (Laughlin preferred just "J"), had decided to pursue publishing. Laughlin had a passion for new, up-and-coming poets, so his publishing company, New Directions, concentrated on helping bring such writers to prominence. He had the perfect footing with which to support starving poets: inherited wealth. For Tennessee, a friend in publishing was a friend indeed, and they would remain close. Laughlin was one of few individuals who could unequivocally call Williams a friend, without having a falling out, in his or Williams' lifetime.

If one is to read the letters from this 1941-42 time period, it seems that Tennessee lived an action-packed life in the space of only a couple of years. He stayed with friends, visited contemporaries, and crashed in all manner of residences. It truly is amazing the adventures he went on, stopping by home every once in a while like a hero blowing back into port. Edwina and Rose always awaited the return of the prodigal from his adventures, while Cornelius was (at least psychically) living a life apart, and Dakin was making a way for himself.

His absence would come at a cost, though: in January of 1943, after increasing incidents at home and in public, Edwina had endured enough of what she considered Rose's demented antics. Something had to be done to cease Rose's indecent ramblings—discussions of topics her mother considered perverse. A specialist recommended a treatment for Rose, which Edwina consented to. She rallied support from Cornelius, also disposed to subjecting Rose to a procedure that would no longer be practiced only a few short years later. It was then, while Tom was off gallivanting and living his charmed life that a bilateral prefrontal lobotomy was performed on Rose. She would never be the same. He was not told about the procedure until after it had taken place. He would never forgive himself.

Could he have prevented the operation if he had known about it? Could he have helped Rose if he had been more attuned to her plight? If he had been around more? If they had kept better correspondence? If he had an opportunity to reason with his parents, both of whom had to agree to the operation? These and many other questions would haunt Williams for the rest of his life. They would resurface and inform the themes and action of his plays, poems, and stories. Dozens of references to roses, often crushed in some cruel and ambivalent way, appear in his plays. Questions of responsibility and consequences for absence are posed by numerous characters in his collected works.

In a moment, the young writer who began by fabricating essay answers and Egyptian fantasy from no real knowledge of the subject became concerned with distilling truth into imagined circumstances. He understood now that writing from his own knowledge and experience—while converting details into composite form—was not just necessary to commune with the audience, but also to work out his own inner turmoil. This painful, traumatic circumstance forged a playwright of intense introspection.

That playwright is *the* Tennessee Williams.

Points of Interest

- *Battle of Angels* opens on December 30 in Boston, Massachusetts, and closes after only two weeks in January of 1941.
- Williams spends much of 1941 and 1942 traveling, honing his craft, and coping with various creative and personal explorations.
- In late 1942, Williams meets James Laughlin of New Directions Publishing.
- In January of 1943, a bilateral prefrontal lobotomy is performed on Williams' sister, Rose.

THE SCENIC ROUTE

Before adopting the moniker "Tennessee" for good, Tom Williams turned out a series of plays in the amateur and college settings. Several of them have been mentioned—*Stairs to the Roof, Candles to the Sun, Fugitive Kind*—and each of them had sociopolitical messages. While under Dr. Mabie at the University of Iowa, Williams was coaxed to write plays that made statements, but the most interesting messages to Williams were always personal ones. Mabie struck down *Spring Storm,* a character-driven drama, but perhaps it's because he was trying to push Tom toward other genres. One assignment that Williams was given in the writing program was to make a Living Newspaper-style play. Living Newspaper was a type of theatre in which the play presents current events in an accessible way for audiences. It was a mainstay of the Federal Theatre Project. Mabie assigned his students to present such a play, and Williams' offering was *Not About Nightingales.*

Nightingales is a play set in a prison on the eve of a hunger strike. The prisoners, furious over the poor conditions and even worse food, attempt to take the warden to task, demanding better treatment. The warden is unwilling to budge, and opts to torture the revolting inmates by locking them in a boiler room to sweat until they succumb to his whims. Some of the men in the steamy compartment suffocate or burn to death. The ringleader of the prisoners escapes, and with the help of the warden's inmate assistant, Jim, exacts revenge on the tyrant. There is also a romantic subplot involving Jim and the warden's new secretary, Eva, which ends almost as tragically as the warden's own downfall.

The play was loosely based on a real-life hunger strike, which ended in inmates in a Pennsylvania prison suffocating after being tortured in a boiler room. *Nightingales* is one of Williams' most socially driven plays, numbering among those others from this period. Even with its hard-hitting intent of shining a light on injustice to the incarcerated, Williams was concerned with the personal, interior drama. He added human touches to the warden and Butch, and presented a fully fleshed-out Jim and Eva story. Each character had complex, intense histories that were completely explored through dialogue. As Williams returned to his character-driven mode of playwriting with *Battle of Angels,* echoes of *Nightingales, Candles, Stairs,* and *Fugitive Kind* would resurface. Moving forward, he would largely de-emphasize overt social causes in favor of crafting more emotionally resonant scenarios.

IV

THE PEAK OF BLUE MOUNTAIN

Points of Interest

- Williams spends the years following *Battle of Angels* working and re-working a multitude of short plays, long plays, short stories, and poems.
- Williams is sent to California in 1943 by Audrey Wood to take up work for Metro-Goldwyn-Mayer Studios (MGM).
- In the same year, Williams begins reworking a play called *The Gentleman Caller,* which is a culmination of several sketches and shorter works dating back to 1938.
- *You Touched Me!,* a play co-authored by Williams and his friend Donald Windham, opens in Cleveland.

In the years following *Battle of Angels,* Williams' family life and travels could have filled volumes of biography on their own. Running parallel to those events, Tennessee continued to write unendingly. You'll remember that I mentioned before that

Williams wrote a lot. I believe the words I used were "a lot, a lot." During his guest room odyssey, he was in constant correspondence with friends that were poets and show business folk, particularly gay men he'd met in his travels, primarily in New York. The constellation of pals comprised Oliver Evans, Paul Bigelow, Gilbert Maxwell, and distinctly significant to this period was another young, promising writer named Donald Windham. In addition to a love for writing, the boys bonded over their mutual love of men, sharp humor, camp, and compulsive revision of their work. Over the years, Windham collected his correspondence with Tennessee and composed a volume, and dozens of Tennessee's letters to the other gents can be found in other books. Alongside Williams' journals, these "secret" writings are an illuminating study into gay language and humor in mid-twentieth century America. They involve coded language, camp, and even what may be one of the earliest iterations of "<u>Girl</u>!" used as an exclamatory.

Amid the camp, Williams and Windham did plenty of work. They helped one another with revisions and wrote a play together called *You Touched Me!,* based on a story by the same name by D. H. Lawrence. During Williams' first cross-country trip with Jim Parrot back in 1939, the boys had stopped off to visit Frieda Lawrence, the famous novelist's widow, and she became fond of Williams, so adapting the work was not an issue when the time came to approach Lawrence's estate: she was a pal. The work on *You Touched Me!* was ongoing, and more than once got shelved for other campaigns. Through patience and collaboration, however, the fellows did eventually pull it off. Williams revisited Lawrence's life and works more than once for inspiration, and the poet and his material are more prevalent in Williams' works than any other: in *Adam and Eve on a Ferry, I Rise in Flame, Cried the Phoenix,* and the aforementioned *You Touched Me!,* plus a distinct mention of "that insane Mr. Lawrence" in *The Glass Menagerie,* an author whose book the puritanical Amanda cannot abide having in her home.

During his prolonged creative walkabout, Williams was working on his own individual writing, too. He generated several short plays that juxtaposed the magical world outside of toil against mundane labor. The long play *Stairs to the Roof* is a fantasy on this topic, and Williams shopped it around for quite some time, always to the same response. It was a little too far out to hit home for folks . . . at the time. He crafted short stories of his mythical South with its desperate heroines and secret hedonists. Since the late 1930s, though, there was a subject he continuously revisited: the notion of a fragile woman whose personality was too gentle or pure for the ambivalent universe around her. These works bore titles such as *If You Breathe, It Breaks,* "Portrait of a Girl in Glass," *Daughter of the American Revolution: A Dramatic Portrait of an American Mother (A Comedy),* and eventually *The Gentleman Caller.*

This habitual re-working of fragments and ancestors of evolving works finally tied directly into Rose's woeful circumstance in the most unlikely of places—a movie studio. In the late spring of 1943, Audrey called Tennessee to New York. She had a job for him, this time in California. The contract was with Metro-Goldwyn-Mayer, or MGM Studios. This was one of the giants of film production until about the dawning the digital age. The contract for the writer (Williams) would attach him to an assigned actor, and the screenwriter would be responsible for writing material for said actor. Williams' initial assignment was to craft what he termed "a celluloid brassiere for Lana Turner." To break that down a little, celluloid is the film material on which movies were recorded. Accordingly, Tennessee felt his job was to write a movie to support the starlet's tits. After a short spell trying to make it work for Turner, the studio decided the child star Margaret O'Brien might be more Tennessee's speed, and reassigned him.

Part of the reason Tennessee wasn't delivering for the studio—aside from the fact that he saw the assignment as asinine—was that he was busy working and re-working of his more fulfilling material. That's where *The Gentleman Caller* makes its entrance. At one point during his short tenure at MGM, before being dismissed for professional and aesthetic shortcomings, he pitched the screenplay he had adapted from his stories. MGM rejected it, and Tennessee went back to revisions on it. By this point, he was sure there was something there, and the therapeutic value of writing Laura, Tom, and Amanda was too great to set down.

Through his work on *The Gentleman Caller,* Tennessee was unpacking and making some small peace with the St. Louis situation. It helped him to cope having composites of a domineering but well-meaning mother; a fragile, deep-feeling sister; and a stifled son on the way out the door. While they aren't identical to the historical figures of Edwina, Rose, and Tennessee Williams, they were drawn closely enough from life to be particularly poignant and significant to him. Regardless of the personal import carried by *The Gentleman Caller,* it did not translate to anything MGM could use. While Williams was psychologically unpacking, he was concurrently packing his bags for his exit from MGM. The studio did not renew his contract after six months.

Turned out by the movie people, it might have been the end for Tennessee, but he continued to show tenacity. He worked feverishly on *The Gentleman Caller* and *You Touched Me!,* and in October 1943 the latter finally had its life onstage. Windham and Williams' adaptation of the Lawrence story premiered at the Cleveland Playhouse. It had been workshopped out of town at the Pasadena Playhouse under the astute direction of a Texas firebrand named Margo Jones. Williams and Jones became fast friends during the process. Margo saw Tennessee's time at MGM as a means to an end, and was dead set upon ensuring his place as a titan of theatre. She quickly became one of the keepers of the faith that surrounded Williams in his creative endeavors, flanked by other vital supporters like Edwina (warts and all), Audrey Wood, and incidentally Molly Thacher.

Unlike its workshopping in Pasadena by Margo, the Cleveland production was directed into a pitiful product, and Margo relayed the news. Williams skipped the Cleveland production. Things seemed to be shaking apart for Williams again with the disintegration of the MGM deal, the poor showing of *You Touched Me!,* and temporary souring of relations with his good friend Donald over the collaborative process. It was time for Williams to head back east and once again pick up the pieces of his creative and human endeavors. He took some time to close up shop in California, seeing Margo's version of *You Touched Me!,* and visiting with Laughlin and other friends before popping in on Frieda Lawrence in Taos en route to St. Louis for Christmas.

The year 1944 started rockily. One of Williams' most steadfast supporters, his grandmother, whom he called Grand, died of a long illness on January 6 in her daughter's arms; her husband the Reverend crouched praying by her side. Upon returning from a trip and learning of Mrs. Dakin's death, Cornelius, who was always cast as a villain, was struck by a grief so deep and sincere that it shocked the whole family. The Williamses and Reverend Dakin mourned their matriarch for the coming months, during which Tennessee remained with them in St. Louis. There he continued to write through his mourning and correspond with his writer friends. That spring, he picked up shop and returned to New York, only to immediately find that Kip Kiernan, his first actualized love, had fallen ill. In a matter of days, Kip, too, died on Tennessee.

In a fog of grief that miraculously did not mar his creativity, Williams received one bright beacon: another grant to spur his work. The American Academy of Arts and Letters provided him with a thousand dollars, and that was enough to fund a retreat back up to Provincetown while he processed his losses and continued to work, mostly on plays. He decided to complete *The Gentleman Caller* that summer. He showed up in P-Town at approximately the eve of D-Day. The town was abuzz with nervous excitement, seasoned with trepidation.

Meanwhile in California, Margo was plugging away at one of the plays Tennessee had shared with her to chew on called *The Purification.* She was still determined to blaze Tennessee's trail toward theatrical stardom. At the same time, Tennessee had someone doing similar work on the poetic front for him: James Laughlin twice included Tennessee's work in his publications. Despite the crippling blows of the past couple of years, there were angels guarding Tennessee.

It was his chief angel Audrey that broke the ceiling into the heavens, it would seem. In September of 1944, just after Tennessee returned to New York,

Audrey handed over a copy of *The Gentleman Caller* to an actor-producer named Eddie Dowling. Dowling convinced the producer Louis J. Singer to make the play happen. To add star power, they recruited the semi-retired grande dame Laurette Taylor to play the lead, Amanda. Actress Julie Haydon, the girlfriend of an influential critic, was selected to play the unconventional ingenue Laura. Dowling saw himself in the lead role of Tom. In a flash, *The Gentleman Caller* was nearly cast and certainly happening. Further, the magic word was being floated: *Broadway.*

Dowling's ambition and the speed with which he set the producing machine into motion took Williams by surprise. In all his years of writing, he had never been catapulted to so advanced a stage of talks so quickly. Audrey was ready, though, and kept in step with Dowling, Singer, and company. Tennessee, seeing the immensity of the situation, pulled in someone he loved and trusted unequivocally. He recommended Margo to assistant direct, and Dowling acquiesced.

Within a month, word of *The Glass Menagerie,* the new title for the play, was in the papers, thanks to the critic whose girlfriend was starring. The rehearsal process was tumultuous—Ms. Taylor was unpredictable and frequently inebriated; Dowling wanted to beef up his role; typical diva stuff—but even a rocky rehearsal process drives toward a premier! When Tennessee briefly returned home, he *was* the hero his family had imagined him to be—only now, national renown supported the idea. Williams was contacted by a reporter for the local paper, another aspiring dramatist named William Inge, to talk about his upcoming production.

Suddenly, the show was happening. In its out-of-town tryout in Chicago, amid all the foibles and misadventures that go into producing, somehow Tennessee Williams' play was imminent. The indefatigable mother with her pushy, too-hard love; the son being choked by his day job while he longed to see and write about the world; the young girl who was too soft for the outside world: they were all there, waiting in the wings to step onstage.

And then they did. The lights came up on the Wingfields on December 26, 1944. During a blizzard. The play was poorly attended; exceedingly so. There was no reasonable expectation that such turnout would garner a Broadway run. However . . .

If not for Ashton Stevens and Claudia Cassidy, you may have never heard of *The Glass Menagerie* or Tennessee Williams. Strange, then, that so few know who they are. They were Chicago theatre critics. When *Menagerie* opened during an almost impassible weather emergency, these two critics went multiple times to see the play, over and over. They wrote reviews urging readers to do what they must to see the show. So enchanted were they with the magic that took place in the Wingfield home that ultimately they were able to lure audiences and managed to make *Menagerie* a critical and commercial success. From there, it earned a Broadway transfer.

The rest is history, as they say. The play opened in New York and transformed the American theatre. Williams in an instant became the golden boy of Broadway. Audiences and critics could not wait to see what he turned out next. The play won the Drama Critics' Circle Award for Best Play. After *Menagerie* opened in late March, in short order the play would be published, a number of his short plays were released to hungry readers in the volume *27 Wagons Full of Cotton: And Other One-Act Plays,* and *You Touched Me!* opened on

Broadway to lukewarm reception. Victory in Europe Day came and the United States entered its most economically prosperous moment since before the Depression. Life was good, and so Tennessee was off to his next conquest, which at the time dealt with Mississippi characters and a plantation called Belle Reve . . .

Points of Interest

- In the first half of 1944, Williams' grandmother and his first love, Kip, pass away.
- In the second half of 1944, Williams completes *The Glass Menagerie* and it is quickly picked up for an out-of-town tryout with Broadway aspirations.
- In 1945, *The Glass Menagerie* opens on Broadway. It wins the Drama Critics' Circle Award for Best Play and propels Williams to overnight fame.
- The same year, Williams' plays are published in *27 Wagons Full of Cotton: And Other One-Act Plays.*
- World War II comes to a close after Victory in Europe Day and precipitating victories of the Allied Powers.

Scenic Route

Becoming a theatrical golden boy was probably not what Williams would have expected if you had asked him in those early St. Louis years, clacking away on that secondhand Underwood Portable typewriter. His first few published works were essays and short stories, and most of his literary-type friends knew him for his poetry. He even held late-night poetry writing sessions during his years working at the shoe factory and his time at Washington University. If asked, young Tom Williams would have probably identified his dream career as that of a poet (we can't say for sure, but we have plenty of indicators).

Williams was a poet first, and that informed his dramatic style. He found success and even fame in drama, sure—but poetry was a constant habit, both within and separate from his plays. He wrote multiple characters who were poets, and many of his plays begin with epigraphs from poetry. Dozens of the tenderest moments in his plays bear quotations from other poets; notably one from Browning in *A Streetcar Named Desire* in which Blanche and Mitch learn they have something in common: a dead lover. Williams recognized the transcendent quality in the words of others, and was not afraid to use their words when they could do the job more effectively than he estimated he might.

Aside from his use of other poets' words, he also learned a great deal from their punctuation. Williams' plays are littered with em dashes (—) and en dashes (–) used in a poet-ly rather than a playwright-ly way. He fashions cadence through creative use of these dashes, commas, and periods in a way that very few dramatists do. His punctuation holds space in time, and supports his idea of a new, plastic theatre briefly detailed in his Production Note for *The Glass Menagerie.* His poetic use of punctuation and monologues that read like blank verse littered with repetition and florid description magnify the musicality in his plays, which I only labor to describe in order to highlight the difference between what audiences were seeing at Williams' plays compared to other writers of the time.

Audiences were interested and impressed by the way Williams used language, and were eager to hear more of his unique voice in the theatre. They were about to get it in the form of a violent, musical, masterstroke of drama that lays bare the human spirit and propelled one of the world's most unique cities to global fame.

What may have elevated the material for *The Glass Menagerie* beyond that of *Battle of Angels* just a few years earlier is the deeper personal connection to the characters he wrote. Williams crafted some wild scenarios in his day, but to hear the plot outline of *Menagerie,* you might ask "So what's the big deal?" After all, it's just about a poor family trying to make do; the sister Laura is terrified of socialization so she needs arrangements made by her kooky mother and her surly brother. Brother secretly plans to leave for adventure's sake like a good, red-blooded American boy, but he finds himself pinned by Ma with an ultimatum: get Sister a man and he can go with no strings attached. The stakes are increased for Tom, he finds the first guy he can, and it's—as Amanda would term it—a fiasco. If the play weren't so tender and poignant as often as it is, it could easily be a comedy! After all, so could *Othello* if not for a handkerchief misunderstanding resulting in a pile of bodies.

It's not the scenarios that make Williams' work special. It's his characters. It's his treatment of the people. *Menagerie* is a perennial testament to that statement. But it wasn't so with *Battle,* which had composites of folks he knew, for sure. They were parishioners he visited days long ago with his grandfather on sick visits and townspeople he had met in the Delta and in Tennessee. They weren't family. Not like the Wingfields. Tom, Amanda, and Laura were drawn much more closely and carefully from a pool of characteristics of people he understood deeply. While they aren't photographic likenesses of Edwina or Rose, they had pure, real facets that Williams knew intimately—traces of the real, which brought their truth more into focus onstage. That's the magic potion that Williams happened upon with *Menagerie,* and which he'd work to perfect for the rest of his career. Finally, with all the Egyptian queens and imaginary wives and sailor boys relegated to the distant past, he was writing what works: what he knew.

V

INTO THE WHITE WOODS

Points of Interest

- In 1946, Williams becomes involved with Pancho Rodriguez y Gonzales while living in and traveling from his home base in New Orleans.
- In 1947, the expectation for Williams to release another masterpiece is met with *A Streetcar Named Desire*.
- *Streetcar* is Williams' first collaboration with director Elia Kazan.

New Orleans, Louisiana, is a hell of a town. It's perhaps best known for Jazz music, Mardi Gras, Creole cuisine, a hurricane that caught national attention, and the subsequent football victory that resonated as a Cinderella story. Visitors to the Crescent City may not immediately think of theatre, but when they do, they think of Tennessee Williams. It's with good reason—were it not for Tennessee Williams, New Orleans may not have developed to be one of the most culturally fascinating destinations for folks from all over the world.

In the months following the catapulting success of *The Glass Menagerie*, Williams worked on a play that had a handful of titles in its various iterations: *Spinning Song, Blanche's Chair in the Moon, Interior: Panic,* and the *Poker Night* to name a few. Each sketch of a play had some similar elements—an unravelling debutante, a woman named Blanche, a dangerous game, the plantation Belle Reve, translated from French as "Beautiful Dream" . . . elements from each worked its way into Williams' next big project. (Okay, so, arguably it might be pronounced "bell REEV," which would phonetically translate as "beautiful bank/shore" (belle rive). In French, the word *reve*—dream—is masculine, so it would be named "Beau Reve" . . . Williams was not a French scholar, so we give him a pass.)

If you already possess some knowledge of the "essential" Tennessee Williams, you've probably guessed that these plays evolved into *A Streetcar Named Desire.* It was a natural, resounding answer to the cries from audiences and critics for Williams to craft another blockbuster. It showcased two sides of the South, a region he had already made mythic in the character of Amanda Wingfield. It took place in the sultry, seedy French Quarter—and not the tourists' end—the locals' side. Audiences gobbled up the drama, the setting, and the characters—all flavors they'd never tasted in concert.

The play follows the plight of Blanche DuBois, a down-on-her-luck schoolteacher who spent the last several years inching into spinsterhood while caring for her ailing family. Meanwhile, her sister, Stella, set out on her own and landed in New Orleans, marrying a strapping young guy of Polish ancestry (the "wrong kind" of white folk in the

1940s; otherness was broader back then). When Blanche arrives in the city to stay with Stella, having nowhere else to go, she finds the situation untenable, and herself desperately unable to find other safe harbor. The play highlights the Old South's need to survive when faced with an urbanizing New South that's more diverse and less genteel than the former can cope with.

Beyond a social message, *Streetcar* portrayed human suffering and relationships with harrowing honesty. It has been termed a "tragedy of incomprehension" because the characters' conflicts root not from abject cruelty, but from their inability to understand each other's sensitivities and needs. Audiences, in return, felt seen and understood because of the nuance with which Williams treated his characters and situations. For each measure of violence, there is a soft spot carved out in the play. Each time a lie is told, there is a greater truth that is alluded to. Williams was asking his audience to feel and recognize themselves, and the audiences were eager to do so.

As with *Menagerie,* Willams wasn't pulling this play out of thin air as he did with his apprentice essays and fantasy writings. Instead, he was lifting details from real-life characters and transmogrifying them to completely alive creatures to strut and fret on the stage. The character of Blanche is attributed to Williams' paternal aunt, whom he viewed as a glamorous grande dame with airs, and the name probably came from Blanche Cutrer, a well-known, wealthy member of Clarksdale society with a fancy house in a prominent part of town. Other characters from the play were surely lifted from his interactions with the colorful French Quarter personalities he encountered in his time in New Orleans in 1939 and beyond.

Speaking of beyond, far away from the neon white glow of Broadway, Williams had settled into New Orleans to complete *Streetcar*. While there, he became entangled in a tumultuous relationship with a local named Pancho Rodriguez y Gonzales. Tennessee and Pancho became known far and wide for their passionate carousal and fighting. They were the shouting-match-in-public, scaling-the-sides-of-buildings type of couple. They were fiercely territorial but also only monogam-ish, which proved to be a volatile combination.

The drama in bringing *Streetcar* together was less vitriolic than that on Tennessee's home front, but it was not without the odd bump-and-start. There was even a touch of kismet, like with *Menagerie*. When readying herself to shop the script, Audrey insisted that the play's name be changed at such time as it was still titled *The Poker Night*. Tennessee plunged for other imagery, landing on *A Streetcar Named Desire*. Audrey presented its most complete iteration to a handful of hungry producers. It was Irene Selznick, a theatrical producer and heiress to the Mayer family (the second "M" in "MGM"), who bit. When it came to a director, Williams had been continually impressed by the work of one man, who happened to be husband to Molly Day Thacher (there's your kismet). Elia Kazan is who Tennessee wanted, and that's who he got.

Williams and Kazan would collaborate on half a dozen projects of varying degrees of critical and artistic success—mostly on the highly successful end of the spectrum. For nearly two decades, Kazan was Williams' ideal director, but not every project was a match; not as far as Kazan was concerned. He would take Tennessee up when he felt the project was right, and decline involvement (usually) when he felt the project was outside of his wheelhouse. Their candid cooperative relationship served Kazan to become a stronger director and spurred Williams to make some vital edits to works that otherwise might have been weaker (again, usually). Kazan was one of Williams' creative consciences, and (usually) his critiques were met warmly. Other times, with sparks and scorn.

If his introduction to Kazan were not fortuitous enough, another introduction *from* Kazan was soon to come, and it would be similarly significant. During the summer of 1947, once Kazan was on board, Williams and Pancho elected to visit Provincetown. There are two legends of that summer worth noting. First, while cruising the storied gay watering hole the A-House just off the main drag Commercial Street, Williams engaged in some in-the-dunes hanky-panky with a young Sicilian gent. When Pancho realized what was going on, he allegedly chased the offending Tennessee in his car over the dunes and into the road. The man was named Frank. The second legend is that Kazan sent up from New York an actor to read for the role of Stanley Kowalski (named after a coworker of Tennessee's in St. Louis, and the antagonist to Blanche DuBois in *Streetcar*). The story goes that Marlon Brando arrived, Tennessee was having plumbing issues, and Brando was happy to oblige with fixing the pipes before giving a reading that greatly impressed Tennessee. To be clear, the story is about actual, literal plumbing.

Brando's delivery of the material was good enough to win him the part in the play, and he was paired against Jessica Tandy and Kim Hunter, both names of the day. The endearing character actor Karl Malden rounded out the primary characters in the cast, and *Streetcar*'s success seemed a foregone conclusion under Kazan's expert hand.

It delivered. The *Streetcar* garnered rave reviews, another Drama Critics' Circle Award, and even a Pulitzer Prize. Moreover, it confirmed the strength of Williams and Kazan's collaborative partnership.

While the drama of *Streetcar* was imaginary, the tumult in Williams' relationship with Pancho was not. Shortly after the play opened, the couple split. Almost immediately thereafter, when Williams was on one of his constitutional cruises (the sex kind, not the nautical type), he ran across the handsome, compact Sicilian Frank Merlo again, and they began a relationship that would span fourteen years. With two smash Broadway plays under his belt, a new relationship, and a new collaborative partner in Kazan, Williams was set to begin 1948 on the highest of high notes.

Blanche DuBois's name, she tells the character Mitch, means "white woods." It evokes a mystique and a scenario the man could easily get lost in. Blanche, seemingly unable to help herself, weaves a web of white lies that ensnares Mitch and eventually entangles Blanche herself. Before he realized it, Williams found himself knotted in a kind of web, himself. The themes, topics, and character archetypes through which he had found great triumph soon became boundaries of a genre of his own creation. Without realizing it, the critical success he found on the backs of Southern heroines in desperate situations were becoming the bars of a cage. He had always been an experimentalist, but at this point John Q. Public would not have known it.

His book of one-act plays *27 Wagons Full of Cotton: and Other One-Act Plays* included some offerings readers might not expect, but even its titular play concerns a desperate Southern woman in the Mississippi Delta. Amanda's fictional Blue Mountain smacks of the Delta, too—it's lousy with references that are distinctly Clarksdalian, in spite of the fact that there are no mountains in the Delta (just burial mounds), and there's a real place called Blue Mountain in Northeastern Mississippi. At first glance, one might think that Blanche DuBois's hometown Laurel is the *actual* Laurel, Mississippi, just a stone's throw from New Orleans, really. Instead, it seems it's another Delta composite. Unwittingly, Williams created a territory that he was expected to stay in. Even his representatives expected him to turn out more Southern material.

Summer and Smoke was his next Delta offering to Broadway. Its story follows Alma Winemiller, another Southern spinster who has been bound by responsibility to care for her unwell mother alongside her father, a pastor. Her childhood crush, the neighbor boy, returns to town a newly minted doctor, and she becomes fixated on him. Her struggle is with her own notions of propriety, no matter how hedonistic the young man proves himself to be. The plot culminates in one of the most devastating displays of two ships passing in the night ever to take place on a stage. If I've made it sound interesting, however, that is not how it seemed when it opened on Broadway in the fall of 1948. For all its will-they-or-won't-they longing, its run was not long at all. Its critical reception was chilly and audiences, it might have seemed, were exhibiting signs of belle-fatigue. If the audiences and critics were starting to cool on old Tennessee, it was fortuitous that he was about to shake things up creatively, domestically, and beyond. The 1950s were a decade of increasing momentum for Williams, come what may.

Points of Interest

- A *Streetcar Named Desire* wins a Drama Critics' Circle Award and garners Williams' first Pulitzer Prize.
- Pancho and Tennessee split up, but in early 1948, Williams comes across an acquaintance from before, Frank Merlo. They become partners for fourteen years.
- Elia Kazan and Williams stay in contact for several years, and Kazan becomes one of Williams' creative consultants on many projects.
- *Summer and Smoke* opens on Broadway in October of 1948.

SCENIC ROUTE

Another paradigm shift that *Streetcar* initiated often goes unnoticed. *Streetcar* introduced in the character of Stanley and the body of Brando an erotic fixture that was male, raw, and unapologetic. His compact, chiseled chest and imposing biceps were a counterpoint to his child-like pout and boyish tomfoolery. Men onstage had never been portrayed as feasts for the eyes, and handsome ingenues were certainly never this complicated. In Stanley, Williams set the loins of the masses ablaze, and he did so with a character that in one moment the audience loves and in the next they revile as he rapes Blanche—his wife's sister; while his wife delivers their baby at the time of the assault. As imperfect as his character was, he represented a paradigm shift in how men *could* be portrayed onstage, setting the stage for future Williams plays, Inge plays, and even the charming but problematic himbos of the silver and digital screens.

VI

HOT SOUTH

Points of Interest

- In 1948, Tennessee and Frank set off for Europe, spending time in Italy where they visit Frank's family.
- Williams buys a home in Key West where he relocates along with Frank and the Reverend Dakin in 1949.
- In 1950, *The Roman Spring of Mrs. Stone,* Williams' first published novel is released. In the same year, *The Glass Menagerie* is released as a film by Warner Brothers.
- In 1951, *The Rose Tattoo* opens on Broadway and wins a Tony Award.

In December 1948, Frank convinced Tennessee to take a trip to Europe. Tennessee delighted at the notion, having not been to Europe in ten years. On this trip, concentrated in Italy, Williams met Gore Vidal and Truman Capote, two other gay writers of the day. Both had biting wits and were surrounded by the most beautiful hangers-on and sharpest literary minds. They were charmed by Tennessee, and regarded him in different ways. Based on correspondence and anecdotes, Vidal estimated Williams as a confederate in the trenches of human understanding, though neither was above taking the odd verbal swipe at the other. Capote, on the other hand, saw Williams more as a sparring partner, and Williams tended to feel more like Capote's punching bag. Sometimes the claws came out, but the indelible fact was that all three writers respected one another's place in the pantheon of celebrity queer writers of the day. They would number among Williams' other peers in LGBTQ+ literati alongside William Inge, Donald Windham, Carson McCullers, and Christopher Isherwood, to name only a few.

What struck Williams on this international visit even more than new, brilliant company was the beauty of Italy and its people—particularly Sicilians. For those readers who aren't familiar with the difference, Sicilians are a subculture of Italians, with a handful of considerable differences. **Una deviazione veloce:** All Sicilians are Italian (ethnically and nationally), but not all Italians are Sicilian, as they're not, well . . . from Sicily. Sicilians will let you know if they feel mis-categorized as regular ol' Italians, and vice versa. There are linguistic and culinary differences, as well. Frank Merlo was Sicilian American, so let's **place the button on the detour there.** He visited his relatives with Tennessee, and the poet was bedazzled. Refreshed by the European excursion and inspired by the Italian climes and culture, Tennessee and Frank returned stateside.

As he'd gained prominence and means, Tennessee saw opportunities to care for his family. After Italy, he relocated his aging grandfather to Key West to live with himself and Frank. They spent the rest of the Reverend Dakin's life enjoying the sun and surf together, having drinks with the boys, and enjoying the gay island lifestyle. Note that I do not place a connotation on the word "gay." But I don't *not* put a connotation on it, either. Either way, the old man was happy, and the fellows were glad to give him a free and easy last few years of life.

Williams also saw to Rose's care, though not at his own homestead. She needed closer attention, so he made accommodations for her at a series of facilities throughout the years before finally settling her into the Stony Lodge Clinic in upstate New York. Frank had stepped into the role of secretary for his partner, which freed Williams up to concentrate on his writing and taking care of his loved ones. He was never free of anxiety about what came next, or when his output would suddenly, completely diminish. For years, Williams worried about sliding downhill creatively, but this period in the early 1950s, with Frank as his copilot, he was held aloft.

From their place on Duncan Street, Williams set to work writing stories and plays with a distinctly Italian lean, and focused some of them on the Sicilian characters he'd met on his voyage to Frank's ancestral home. The first fruit of that olive tree was in 1950 with *The Roman Spring of Mrs. Stone,* a novel about an aging actress who imagines—maybe accurately—that her creative career is waning. She meets and becomes infatuated with an Italian hustler on a springtime vacation to Rome, and they have numerous trysts that create opportunities for danger, desire, and probing dialogue, as was Williams' mode. Williams may have been reflecting on his own imagined creative collapse, but the novel did not present any evidence of decline. The specter of perceived degradation couldn't keep the man down, and he kept writing.

Still ruminating on Mediterranean themes and people, Tennessee next produced something funny, touching, and which contains a genuinely happy ending. The year 1951 heralded the opening of *The Rose Tattoo,* a play about a Sicilian American community in coastal Mississippi. It had components of tragedy toward the beginning of the story, but somersaulted into moments of outrageous comedy and romance later in the play. The protagonist Serafina delle Rose is a seamstress who loses her husband in a car accident on the very night she learned he was unfaithful to her. Her grief and unusual way of coping leads her into a protracted, yearslong mourning period in which she convinces herself that he was faithful to her. The fantasy she constructs has a Rapunzel-like effect on her daughter, Rosa, and the play's action picks up on the girl's graduation day, when Serafina is forced to reckon with her child's rebelliousness, the townsfolk clamoring for past-due graduation gowns, and the arrival of several unwanted visitors . . . including a goofy man who reminds her of her husband in all aspects but his clown-like face. The joy and hilarity of the play is impossible for Serafina to contain, and the action blossoms into a glorious climax—for the audience and the character. Fittingly, Williams dedicated the play: *To Frank in return for Sicily.*

Picking a Sicilian enclave of a Southern town was a change for Williams. *Mrs. Stone* takes place in an Italian setting and centers on an American character similar to but older than some of Williams' previous works. Conversely, *Rose Tattoo* concerns an immigrant character and her immigrant community moving among one another and navigating the grotesque racism of the "white" characters. Returning to the earlier

detour, in 1951, Italians, particularly Sicilians, were "not quite white" in the American South, and would remain that way for a couple of decades, depending on what part of the country they found themselves in. This isn't unlike Stanley's standing in *Streetcar,* being denigrated by Blanche for his Polish background. In the Deep South, pockets of various once-othered ethnic groups can still be found, but they've mostly assimilated into other neighborhoods and cultures as the lines have blurred. Even so, New Orleans and the Mississippi Delta still have robust Sicilian populations and all of the unique cultural trappings. To tie the **detour** back to the main road, these Italian characters boldly introduced Williams' interest in characters grappling with the otherness of ethnicity. *The Rose Tattoo* was one of several times that Williams would confront the South's overt racism.

Tattoo won a Tony Award for Best Play, and its star Maureen Stapleton was lauded for her portrayal of Serafina (at age 25!). Williams had been courting Italian actress Anna Magnani for the role (which she portrays in the film adaptation) for several months, but the diva's talent was no match for her fear. She worried that she wouldn't be able to deliver the English lines with adequate gusto. Nineteen fifty-one was a good year to be America's greatest playwright. In addition to snagging a Tony Award, it was also the year that *A Streetcar Named Desire* received its life on the silver screen. It starred much of the original cast: Kim Hunter and Karl Malden as Stella and Mitch, respectively . . . and, of course, Brando's portrayal of Stanley and his biceps and sultry pout were blazed into the psyches and loins of audiences around the globe. This was seismic.

Points of Interest

- In 1950, *The Glass Menagerie* is adapted for film and released.
- In 1951, Elia Kazan directs the screen version of *A Streetcar Named Desire* starring Vivien Leigh as Blanche.
- In 1952, director José Quintero revives *Summer and Smoke* to great acclaim at Circle in the Square Theatre in New York.
- In 1953, *Camino Real* opens on Broadway to disastrous reviews and closes shortly after.

The impact a large-scale release of *Streetcar* had on the planet's human population can't be ignored. There is no metric for the significance of a singular cultural event's impact on the global zeitgeist, to be sure. The evidence is anecdotal, yet I would still venture to say that the societal permanence of *Streetcar* was spurred most significantly because of its wide film release. The work's potency then spread from home viewing availability, trickling down to various high school, college, and community stage productions. The impact of *Streetcar* becoming part of the global zeitgeist caused continual ripples in the world theatre scene and likely influenced how audiences viewed some of the topics covered and themes dissected in the material. The eroticizing of the male figure is prominent among new territories explored. The treatment of a desperate, deeply flawed woman was nothing new, but audiences profess to this day to be stunned by the naked emotional truth of Blanche DuBois. The film also shone a spotlight on its setting: New Orleans. Without its release, it might have been years before another writer showcased one of the world's most interesting cities. Last, it portrayed Southernness (Southernity?) as a complex spectrum, rather than the black-and-white white-folk-and-Black-folk trope exercised so frequently before. Stanley's South is at odds with Blanche's South. The urban, progressive sprawl of Creole New Orleans glares over its border, which is intimidating to the "Old Dixie" South. In New Orleans, Blanche is faced with Black people who—gasp!—*do not work for her.* Williams did as much as he could to shear off the genteel veneer of the South as it had been exhibited in earlier works.

Just a year prior, *The Glass Menagerie* had been adapted to a film featuring Gertrude Lawrence and Kirk Douglas, but thanks to censors and changes, it lacked the heart of the stage production. When placed against the film adaptation of *Streetcar,* the material in *Menagerie,* well . . . it blanched in comparison. So easily overshadowed was the *Menagerie* film that even some Williams fans don't know it happened, or when.

While an Off-Broadway production of *Summer and Smoke* was being staged by visionary director José Quintero, Williams was busy working and reworking a play he had been tinkering with for ages: *Ten Blocks on the Camino Real.* He insisted in the first page of the script that the title be read in the jarring, Anglicized way, emphasizing the pronunciation *Real,* rather than wray-*ahl.* He wanted to show the world what it's like to tread the *real* road, not the romanticized Royal Road. He could think of no better director to pack up and hit that trail with than Elia Kazan, who had already proven his mettle on the stage and film versions of *Streetcar.*

Over months of revisions and reworking, Williams and Kazan collaborated to craft *Camino Real*— now it featured sixteen "blocks," which amount to scenes or vignettes, and the story beggars the tongue and keypad to explain. So I'll try just that:

The play begins with Don Quixote and Sancho

Panza from the epic novel by Miguel de Cervantes approaching the gates of a dodgy city. Sancho ditches the Don, and the old knight decides to take a nap, prior to which he explains to the audience in no uncertain terms that he will dream a fantasy. That fantasy is what is enacted onstage, and the meta-theatrical convention is established. The town becomes flooded with vagrants, scalawags, and grifters. There are even a few odd rich tourists (or so they seem) punctuating the string of weirdos. Soon after the city is thoroughly populated by the figments of the knight's imagination, the town's boss man and proprietor of the single opulent hotel appears to explain the rough elements and circumstances of the town that sits on the Camino Real.

Next, a young veteran, fresh off a boat appears, full of bluster and optimism. His name is Kilroy, and his optimism quickly gives way to suspicion when he's propositioned, pickpocketed, and pummeled by the police in rapid succession. The remainder of the play follows Kilroy's navigation of the rough dealings on the Camino Real. It involves seedy flophouse bargaining, murder, disposal of bodies by municipal servants, a Gypsy's daughter bait-and-switch scenario, and a plethora of historical and literary characters. Lord Byron walks alongside Camille and Casanova. There's an attempted escape from the purgatorial haven. Heartbreak. Chase scenes. In the end, Don Quixote awakens to restore everyone's faith in humanity and sense of wonder, saving Kilroy from the clutches of those who would rend his American splendor asunder. It sounds like a mess, but when done right, the play is really nice. It's one of those surreal experiences wherein you must let the play happen to you rather than trying to fix yourself onto a literal, linear narrative.

The critics in 1953 did not see it that way. They panned it. I mean, they *paaaaaaaaaanned* it. With several *A*s. Williams took a ribbing from just about every outlet of significance. In retrospect, Kazan admitted that the play was beyond his reckoning. For the critics, the easy direction to point in was backward: Williams had produced such touching, tight dramas about the American South. Why had he not stayed in his lane, and delivered another set of nervous belles? What is this pseudo-Mexican nonsense? Why are they saying the title wrong? And worst, perhaps, was that there was a frank, sexualized portrayal of a gay man onstage in the personage of the Baron de Charlus. The character is borrowed from Marcel Proust's *Remembrance of Things Past,* and he proudly cruises, books a room, and is pleasured by a hustler before being murdered by the same man. As Williams wrote in his journal, "<u>Girl!</u>" That would not do on Broadway.

Brutal Broadway wore Williams out over *Camino,* but it appeared willing to forgive him if he returned to them with something more his speed, in their estimation (the "they" here are the critics as well as audiences—some of whom intimated that they loved the play, but understood its status as an aberration). In short order, Williams would deliver what they were hungry for—a return to the South, and the burning heat of Delta desire.

SCENIC ROUTE

I really have to hand it to Vivien Leigh. Nothing against the lady, and her performance of Blanche in the film version of *A Streetcar Named Desire* was inspired, but she really ruined Tennessee Williams for every other director, actor, audience member, and critic, bless her heart. Her performance was so memorable that audiences remembered Blanche as an epitome of the Southern heroine, which is exactly what she is not. Blanche is a liar and a pedophile, both of which pieces are so unweighted in the screen adaptation of *Streetcar*. For every ounce of heartache she has endured, she has also perpetrated unspeakable acts. Leigh's Blanche buried these notions deep in the subtext—so deep they're nearly obscured. What you have instead is Scarlett Redux—a soft woman who is tough as nails when she needs to be, but who perhaps does not deliver on Blanche's heat and fury. What we know is that the censors had a field day with the screenplay. The clearest evidence of censorship is that Stanley gets his comeuppance at the end of the film: Stella and the baby leave him. By contrast, he is forgiven at the end of the play and the family stays together. Maybe censorship is why Blanche couldn't be as hot and bothersome as she is in the stage play.

Leigh also brought to Blanche an accent that was no part Mississippian. Instead, she recycled her *Gone With the Wind* accent, which smacked of Charleston, South Carolina. Lilting and legato, it definitely had music, and for a woman born in India and raised in England, Leigh did a remarkable job with the voice and the role. Remarkable, too, was that its music—that particular Mississippi Mouth Magic—was absent. The reason I bring this into the discussion is that Williams was astutely attuned to the musicality of human voices and accents. Examples of him phoneticizing words in his plays abound. That's why I have a hard time letting go of the idea that the iconic, set-in-celluloid performance of Blanche is one from another region. In Mississippi, for example, we say our damn *R*s. Brilliant Viv; she did not. Now, we circle to the finale.

So why dissect so painstakingly a performance which was good? What's the point of all this? It's because gradually, the impulse to imitate Vivien Leigh should be set aside. Actors imitate movies. A lot. I'd go so far as to say a lot, a lot. Often it's innocent and well-meaning, but Vivien Leigh's portrayal of Blanche has trickled down for decades into community theatres, regional theatres, schools, and even episodes of popular television shows. The one shot we had at presenting perhaps the most incredible and complex character ever to be produced from Mississippi, and we let a British lady feigning a Carolina dialect tell us all to be demure, soft ladies. Now when I hear folks audition using Blanche, I steadily see women presenting a character devoid of grit, desire, and—well, heat.

VII

Cotton Kingdom

Points of Interest

- *Cat on a Hot Tin Roof* marks another collaboration with Kazan, another Drama Critics' Circle Award, and another Pulitzer Prize in 1955.
- In the same year, the Reverend Dakin passes away.
- Williams and Kazan work together again on the film *Baby Doll* set in the Mississippi Delta in 1956.
- *Orpheus Descending* opens in 1957, continuing a streak of Delta-centered stories.

Cat on a Hot Tin Roof caps the "Big Three" Tennessee Williams plays. It was the second of the three to be directed by Kazan, with *Menagerie* being the only un-Kazan-ed masterwork. *Streetcar, Menagerie,* and *Cat* all deal in some way with Delta women, past or present. The women in Williams' Delta plays had traditionally fallen into the categories of firebrands or standard-bearers. The latter upheld the mores of the Old South: Amanda, Alma Winemiller, Blanche, and the town women in *Battle of Angels* to name several. The firebrands burned too brightly for their environments. These were the table-shakers. By the end of *Summer and Smoke,* Alma has transformed from a standard-bearer into a firebrand (spoiler), and even Blanche shows signs of burning up in Laurel before she appeared in New Orleans, ready to present herself as an agent of the legitimate Old South. In *Battle,* Cassandra Whiteside was the town's firebrand. Williams' fixation on women upholding the old world order while they had a tiny ember smoldering, waiting to incinerate the whole system was likely born of his exposure to Henrik Ibsen and his adoration of Anton Chekhov (There's plenty more about this in Appendix Y!).

One Williams firebrand that stands out among all Williams characters is forever blazed into a generation's memory in the sultry form of Elizabeth Taylor as Maggie, "the Cat." The moniker, like the sensuous gaze of the character herself, sizzles. In the pages of the play, readers encounter a woman that could withstand a nuclear holocaust, only to emerge having used the inferno to light a cigarette. Maggie marks a turning point in Williams' women: they become less apologetic and therefore simultaneously more reviled by other characters and more victorious for it.

Cat also marked a turning point in Williams' dealing with gay characters. In *Camino Real,* the death of the obviously gay (and fabulous) Baron de Charlus satisfied the need for "immorality" to be punished when he becomes the victim of a fatal hustler. Campy and killed: that seemed to make a gay character palatable. With *Cat,* the gay characters are all dead, but none of them are campy comic relief. That was huge in 1955. Skipper, Jack Straw, and Peter Ochello are all characters acknowledged to be gay, and each of them is treated with care and compassion by the better angels of the cast of living characters.

The setting of the drama is the bedroom shared by Maggie and her husband, Brick, who's drunk himself to the verge of impotence. Maggie knows that it's because Brick received a call from his best friend, Skipper, who confessed his love of Brick. When Brick was unable to return the love, Skipper killed himself, and the guilt has led Brick to self-medicate up until the rise of the curtain. Maggie, firebrand that she is, refuses to accept Brick's diminution into a drunkard's grave, and uses her every wile and wit to excite her husband on the bed once shared by Jack Straw and Peter Ochello, the gay men who left Brick's family the house they enjoyed in the first place.

The home now belongs to Big Daddy Pollitt, Brick's father. Big Daddy sees Brick's fast decay, and worries that if Brick doesn't step up, Big Daddy will have to turn over the keys to the kingdom to his dimwitted other son, Gooper. This would be an affront to the kingdom Straw, Ochello, and Big Daddy worked so hard to create and sustain. To compound the urgency of Brick's intervention, the specter of death looms over the Pollitt plantation. Big Daddy receives news late in the play that he'll soon be dead from cancer; other characters having dreaded this likely prognosis all along. In a moment reminiscent of King Lear, Big Daddy rages on the roof in a storm against the outrageous fate he's faced with and his agony at the family's lack of cohesion. *Cat* stands out as one of Williams' only full-length plays that takes place entirely in the time elapsed from curtain to curtain.

Maggie's tenacity ultimately holds the family together (we hope), as she pins her husband into a corner and sinks her teeth into the future. The electrifying drama earned Williams another Drama Critics' Circle Award and his second Pulitzer Prize. Plus, it redeemed him from the stink-eye parade he endured after *Camino Real* confused the masses. Barbara Bel Geddes and Ben Gazzara starred in the Broadway production as Maggie and Brick, respectively, but within a couple years' time the film version was released starring Elizabeth Taylor and Paul Newman. Taylor and Newman became the iconic couple, their Technicolor glamor all but usurping Vivien Leigh and Marlon Brando as the international ambassadors of Williams' signature Southern heat. Burl Ives, a folk singer who discovered a talent for acting, played Big Daddy both on Broadway and in the film. Taylor's white-slip-clad form and bedroom glare have enticed millions to enter the Ochello-Straw bedroom, another testament to the power that the widely-released films are responsible for pollinating Williams' vision of the South around the globe.

I take a moment now, since we're about to depart this cotton field for another, to have a **mini-detour** that will not be much of a detour at all; more like **pulling over to tell the kids in the back to calm down.** You'll notice I don't number Brick among the characters in *Cat* that I label gay. Williams seemed to vacillate on Brick's sexuality, too. All I have is this: there's nothing in the text that says that Brick decidedly *is* or *isn't* gay. Period. Actors and directors can come up with justifications until they're blue in the face, but there is no definitive way to perform the role, to produce it, or to direct it. That's what makes it a play and not a novel. Take Tom Wingfield as another example. He's going out each night to the movies, sneaking in at all hours, getting drunk, planning an escape . . . these are all true facts given to us in the dialogue and stage directions. If a director or actor wants to *infer* that Tom is out cruising or making use of the big tub of popcorn (ask your parents), that's all very well and good. If that's what's needed to make the story make sense for that individual, sure; fine; okay, whatever. It does *not* mean that Tom or Brick's gayness is inherent, and it especially does not mean that it is integral to a cohesive or relevant production. End of story. A director, actor, critic, and others who feels the need to put a deep handprint on the production and co-author does no one any favors. Therefore, I leave it up to you, dear reader, to decide what exactly is Brick's damage vis-à-vis Skipper. Meanwhile, there is plainly stated mention of the sexuality of several characters in dialogue and stage business for the Baron, Allan Grey, Jack Straw, Peter Ochello, and others. **End detour.**

Now back to the Delta cotton fields. Big Daddy's plantation on "twenty-eight thousand acres of the richest land this side of the valley Nile" was one of a few contentious patches of farmland featured in Williams' dramatic oeuvre. Another patch of cotton that helped mythologize the dirty South is in the film *Baby Doll.* The movie was first conceived in the pages of *27 Wagons Full of Cotton,* a short play concerning a dissatisfied housewife who humiliates her prideful, lecherous husband by having a tryst with the man who now holds sway over the local cotton trade. *Baby Doll* grew out of that situation peppered with *The Unsatisfactory Supper,* another Williams one-act. Shot just ten miles from my childhood home in Benoit, Mississippi, *Baby Doll* was another Williams-Kazan collaboration (If you're keeping count, that's five by this point: film and stage productions for *Streetcar,* stage for *Cat* and *Camino,* and now *Baby Doll*).

The fully realized *Baby Doll* centers on Archie Lee Meighan, played by Williams-and-Kazan veteran Karl Malden (Mitch in *Streetcar,* both versions) whose young (*young,* young) wife, "Baby Doll," has promised to consummate their marriage when she comes of age, in exchange for a nicely furnished home that Archie promised Baby Doll's father would be provided for the girl. Archie Lee has failed to provide his terms, and Baby Doll is withholding her end of the bargain, too. Archie Lee becomes excruciatingly frustrated as the promised day draws closer, and he's further exasperated when his cotton business is jeopardized and a shady character shows up at his door offering relief. The shady character is Silva Vacarro, a—*Heavens!*—sexy Sicilian. When Silva meets Baby Doll, matters get worse, as the budding sprite sees in him a more palatable partner than the ogling, ogreish Archie Lee. A struggle ensues for the soul (read: virginity) of Baby Doll, played by the pouting, alluring Carrol Baker (herself *not* a minor, thank heavens). Archie Lee is left a cuckold. Baby Doll is fought over like a piece of property (a baby doll, if you will), and it's never entirely clear if Silva is interested in her body, her mind, or leverage to stick it to Archie Lee. By the time the film hit the screens, Baby Doll had been aged up to 20, but the trailers salaciously and sensationally suggested she was underage.

With minimal violence and an average level of sexual innuendo for a Williams film, *Baby Doll* received a shockingly harsh reception by conservatives in the United States. Priests camped out in movie theatre lobbies to take down the names of parishioners attending the sinful picture at the suggestion of Cardinal Francis Spellman. Meanwhile, over Times Square, Carrol Baker's horizontal body loomed thumb-sucking, framed in a too-small baby's crib across a giant block-long advertisement. Needless to say, moviegoers were hot, damned. It left the church mad out of its cotton-picking mind. Okay, I'll cease the puns now.

It wasn't all cotton and hot sun in 1957, though, as before the end of the year Williams saw his first book of poetry published entitled *In the Winter of Cities,* a decidedly cooler bit of material than all of the Delta plays (okay, last pun. Promise). Having his poems compiled and published was a seminal moment for the writer, since he was always a poet first, and his poetic conscience was his foremost voice. Unlike this writer's puns, Williams' poetry is wonderful, and I encourage your reading of it.

From the *Winter of Cities,* Williams' next large-scale endeavor was another Delta play, itself taking place in winter. *Orpheus Descending* is a more nuanced, mature imagining born from the story of *Battle of Angels,* Williams' traumatic flop of 1940. It has its share of firebrands, standard-bearers, small town ogres and trolls, and, of course, an eroticized male body at the center of its myriad conflicts.

Myra from *Battle* has been reincarnated as Lady Torrance. She's still married to Jabe, a vicious, racist, misogynist hacking his lungs up on the way to dusty death. He brags that he bought Lady at a "fire sale," after wedding her shortly after he and his buddies in the Ku Klux Klan burned up her father's vineyard . . . with her Papa inside. Lady and her father, you see, are wops, which is an outdated, contemptuous epithet for Italians meaning WithOut Papers, describing their immigration situations. Aside from being "dirty" Italians, the family made its money bootlegging (illegally distilling liquor), but they made a fatal "mistake" when they sold booze to Black people. Enter the Klan to deliver swift retribution.

The household and indeed the whole town bears the scars of this original sin that left the beautiful vineyard incinerated and sentenced Lady into Jabe's marriage bed for financial security. Years have passed, and the town shows some small signs of progressing past its wicked history. The town's most prominent heiress Carol Cutrere (named after that famous family in Clarksdale) spent her youth as a race crusader and has evolved into a town pariah because of it. She's looked down upon by everyone except Lady, a person of relative color herself. Carol resembles the punks of the 1970s and '80s, but a few decades early. She's an iconoclast that spits in the face of the power structure, wears wild makeup and hair, and is unbothered by the vitriol aimed at her. She's one of Williams' most brazen firebrands.

As Jabe's power over Lady and his grip on her comings and goings dissolves, mirroring his health, Lady has taken the opportunity to spiff up the shop they own. She is suspicious of his dubious involvement with her family's tragedy all those years ago, and she aims to pay homage to the vineyard by adding a confectionary decorated like a vineyard and symbolizing life to their property. Jabe can't much object; he's languishing with lung disease.

If the circumstances already set forth aren't dramatic enough, a new complication makes the play even more delicious. Valentine Xavier rolls into town to set all the ladies' bosoms ablaze. He's a musician in this rendition, rather than the poet he was in *Battle*. A kind of Elvis of pelvic magnetism, Val is a mystery to everyone in town except Carol— she seems to have his number. She recognizes him as something too rare for the suffocating little town, and begs him to run off with her on several occasions. Carol is a reimagining of Cassandra

Whiteside—and she was a prophet of doom in *Battle* (Cassandra in Greek Mythology is cursed by Apollo for her rejection of his sexual advances. Her curse is to see the future, but never to be believed by others. Williams echoed the prophetic element in Cassandra Whiteside, then with Carol Cutrere).

As Val and Lady predictably fall in love, Val attracts the attention of a few too many ladies married to prominent men in town, and their discontent stirs the sleeping monster in Lady's bed. By the end of the play, Lady is pregnant with Val's baby, ready to open the confectionary and celebrate her heritage just in time for Jabe to come ambling down the stairs to murder her. Val is then restrained and lynched with a blowtorch for having the audacity to be extraordinary in a close-minded village. Only Carol remains of the redeemable characters to light the way to the future.

The epic proportions and allegorical nature of the play are confirmed in its title *Orpheus Descending,* relating it to the Greek myth of Orpheus, demigod and musician, who existed to bring beauty to the undeserving world—only to end up in Hades or ripped apart by horny female spirits, depending on the version of the story.

The play was directed by Broadway titan Harold Clurman, but not even the gods of myth or theatre could save it from a tragically short run. Opening in spring, the production couldn't pull itself from the rainy, muddy Delta winter mire it's first set in. *Orpheus* closed before summer 1957 arrived.

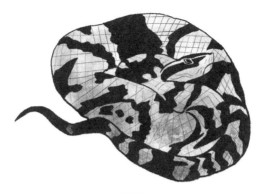

VIII

Caverns Where Monsters Live

Points of Interest

- In 1957, Williams' father dies.
- In 1958, the film version of *Cat on a Hot Tin Roof* is released, and a pair of one acts open Off-Broadway as *Garden District*. The bill features *Suddenly Last Summer* and *Something Unspoken*.
- In 1959, *Sweet Bird of Youth* opens on Broadway.

Jabe Torrance's violence and apathy for the suffering of others probably filtered into Williams' imagination through his father, Cornelius. For much of Williams' life, Cornelius was a perpetrator of cruel treatment: both on Tom's mother and Tom himself. Williams finally began to understand his father as he grew older and used his writing to better understand the human condition. Cornelius died just six days after *Orpheus Descending* opened on Broadway. Cornelius and Edwina had been separated for a number of years, and after leaving

St. Louis, Tennessee had very little contact with his father. Now Tennessee's only close relations included his mother, his brother, and Rose—living on his patronage in a safe place for her condition.

In many areas, Williams' well-being was fracturing. In 1957, he sought out psychotherapy in hopes of surviving a plethora of painful circumstances. *Orpheus*'s failure to launch, Cornelius's death, dismay over what he perceived as his diminishing creative aptitude, a creative blockage, paranoia that he was being professionally alienated, and destabilization of relations between Tennessee and Frank were all contributing factors. He began seeing Dr. Lawrence Kubie for psychoanalysis and boy, oh boy, did it *not work.* To abridge egregiously, two of Kubie's primary recommendations were that Williams pause writing and try not being gay. He did neither. In fact, he doubled down on both.

The output from the psychoanalysis debacle opened Off-Broadway in 1958 with the title *Garden District.* The evening of theatre was composed of two one-act plays: the rarely performed short piece *Something Unspoken* and the often-performed *Suddenly Last Summer,* today considered long enough to be its own night of entertainment. *Something Unspoken* is a tense, compact story about two women who love each other in a power dynamic that makes their love seem perfect to one and frightening to the other. One employs the other; the perch is precarious for the latter.

Garden District's more popular and probing offering was *Suddenly Last Summer.* It's a psychodrama about Violet Venable, a wealthy matriarch living in the richest part of New Orleans. She uses her piles of money and influence to bury the secret of her son's proclivities—particularly pedophilia and homosexuality. Okay, I guess this absolutely calls for a little **detour.** It's recognizable in 2020, as I type these words, that having the only character in a play who is gay also portrayed as a pedophile is problematic to the extreme. After decades of movements meant to push the needle on LGBTQ+ issues, including convincing misguided strangers that queer people are not by virtue of their queerness also perverts, it's troubling to present a night of theatre in which a character is both. It would be like having the only Black actor in a production of *Sweet Bird of Youth* be the same as the one who gives a white character a devastating sexually transmitted infection (white woman being ruined by a Black man—an old Klan trope) or casting Stanley in *Streetcar* with the only Latin actor, resulting in an inadvertent but still problematic machismo/rapist narrative. Yes, theatre makers must consider how they depict marginalized groups when they're monolithic in casting. Fortunately, Mrs. Venable's gay pedophile son is dead for some time before the proverbial curtain goes up, and while his sins are laid bare, so too is a tenderness for his mental instability. The **detour** concludes as we learn that Sebastian's crimes, like problems personal and societal, find a way of growing worse through denial, at least in the world of Tennessee Williams.

Sebastian Venable died in Northern Africa last summer, and Violet has summoned the family to recount the circumstances of his death for a third party. What ensues is part trial, part autopsy. Only one witness remains in whose mind is locked the story of Sebastian's last moments: Catharine Holly, Violet's detested niece. The story Catharine's been reporting does not satisfy Violet's carefully crafted narrative about Sebastian, so she's positioned her niece to sound insane. The judge in the trial situation is a young, ambitious doctor who seems to be part-surgeon and part-psychoanalyst (this is an unusual inconsistency in the play, one must admit). The doctor specializes in lobotomies, which is of unique interest to Violet. If he can be convinced of Catharine's insanity, Violet can pay for the costly procedure and have the hideous story Catharine tells snuffed out forever. Violet's hope is to put out the flame of the firebrand.

In a fraught battle that can certainly be classified as another of Williams' tragedies of incomprehension, Violet sees Catharine as an enemy because she loves her son and needs her life's work protecting him to continue, while Catharine recognizes Violet's pain but cannot let the truth be shut out. Her truth is that Sebastian, out from beneath his mother's supervision, paid young men—some as young as teenagers—for sexual favors, and when he mistreated and degraded them thoroughly, the boys turned on him and literally ate him alive. Naturally, his mother doesn't care for this story.

The imagery of young men eating the senior homosexual, the unfair talk of lobotomizing the heroine, the absence of the man who could stop it, and a series of other personal allegories that Williams figures into *Suddenly* make clear where the real therapy was happening—not in the doctor's office, but on the page. The plays made for riveting theatre, and the Off-Broadway run of *Garden District* was a success—enough so that *Suddenly* was made into a film the next year with a screenplay by Williams' friend and peer Gore Vidal. The play continues to be performed with frequency to this day. Audiences continue to be drawn in by the characters' dueling narratives and the moralism surrounding Sebastian's sins and bizarre absolution.

Before the *Suddenly* film hit the screens, however, *Cat on a Hot Tin Roof* was released in '58, capping off a successful year for Williams. His momentum in the 1950s was strong, even if he stumbled on *Camino* and *Orpheus*. He had an opportunity to work with Kazan again in 1959, so he hoped to cap the decade with another smash. This time, on the collaborative docket, writ large, was *Sweet Bird of Youth*.

Sweet Bird was a new Mississippi play that opened on Broadway under Kazan's adept direction. At the time, it felt contemporary and featured a cast of characters that Williams had seldom put onstage before, though they had existed in his stories and novels. The stars of the action are the Princess Kosmonopolis, alias Alexandra Del Lago, and Chance Wayne. If Chance Wayne strikes you as the name of a hustler, your instinct is dead on. Chance is a hustler becoming long in the tooth. He has latched on to what is very likely to be his last long grift in the personage (and what a personage she is) of the Princess. The Princess is an actress also getting on in years, although she's some years older than Chance. Earlier in the year, she tried for a comeback, but was humiliated into hiding when she saw the close up of her face—aged beyond what she expected to see. Her self-image was not the creature she beheld, and so she's been running ever since, medicating with weed, booze, and hookers to evade reviews and openings. We learn late in the play that her premier was considered a triumph, and her fears were completely unfounded.

As usual, Williams' characters have found themselves in a risky environment in *Sweet Bird*. The two aging creatures that roll into the coastal town inebriated and avoidant have come to a place of special significance. St. Cloud, Mississippi, is

Chance's hometown, a detail he has failed to share with the Princess. He's come by this place on her dime to take care of some unfinished business. After some initial thrashing in which the Princess has some priceless lines calling herself and others monsters, Chance is left to his own devices to bop around town looking for his long-lost lady-love. Her name is Heavenly, because of course it is.

The trouble is, Heavenly remains in body, but she's lost her spirit—and her uterus. The last time Chance blew through St. Cloud, he and Heavenly had a rendezvous, which left her with an unnamed sexually transmitted infection. It went untreated and grew out of control. Having fallen sick, Heavenly needed an operation on her womb. Now, she is in a relationship with the very doctor who performed the surgery. Her father approves of the unusual union, and Heavenly no longer has the willpower to dissent. Now that I bring up her father, it's worth mentioning that he's a prominent politician in the town, and is himself mixed up with the KKK. Williams was not afraid to make villains of the White Knights, so hooray for that.

What doesn't earn a hooray is that Chance gets what Boss Finley, Heavenly's pa, thinks he deserves. He's pinned down and castrated at the end of the play in a weird poetic justice administered by the angry mob. Once the Princess learned that she still had a shot in the pictures, she ditched Chance, leaving him with no real allies or escape plan. *Sweet Bird* is anything but sweet; it's brutal. Violence, regret, and desire were favorite topics explored by Williams and Kazan as a team. The theme of a haunting past stepping inexorably into the present was also something they did well together, as with *Streetcar* and *Cat* (Blanche's indiscretions; Big Daddy's illness). Something being explored this go-round in graphic image and phrases was that there was something from the future coming their way, too—terminus.

In the final speech of *Sweet Bird of Youth,* Chance addresses the audience in a convention that elected to use as a megaphone for the morals of the story. He addresses the battle we all have against an unbeatable enemy, Time. Princess Kosmonopolis escaped to fight another day, but Chance and others represented a fear that Williams had of aging and becoming irrelevant, or worse: having to face the consequences of an imperfect past. As the revenant of age and the fear of the future crept closer to Williams, his relationship to Kazan was becoming more tenuous, too.

They'd been in the trenches together for over a decade, and Tennessee stood beside Elia even in the face of his naming names in the McCarthy hearings when much of the artistic community turned its back on him. While I'd love to reduce the troll to the footnotes of history, it is here that I must explain Joseph McCarthy. Williams experienced some prolonged mistrust and ambivalence in the theatrical and writing community because he kept company with Elia Kazan when the director was brought before the House Un-American Activities Committee, headed by McCarthy. Kazan gave names of socialists during the Red Scare, a witch hunt against marginalized groups and suspected communists (and inspiration for Arthur Miller's *The Crucible*). Kazan was reviled for years for his choice, but Williams kept him as a collaborator—this may have contributed to Williams' apprehension that he had lost some respect by his professional peers.

In spite of Williams' unwillingness to outright ostracize his friend, their styles were becoming simply too disparate. Kazan knew he was whipped by *Camino Real,* and Williams knew that Kazan's help in editing and reworking *Cat* was vital. Nevertheless, the overlapping spheres of what they could work on together were falling farther and farther apart. *Sweet Bird* was the last time Kazan and Williams worked together on a production. They remained in contact and confided in one another for years, but Williams would soon enter a darker place than ever before—and this was one place even Kazan's brilliant dramatic eye could not peer into to save Williams.

The year 1960 delivered two more chilly pieces that seemed to be an answer to the series of burning dramas that led up to it. The film version of *Orpheus Descending* stood out as the collaboration with Anna Magnani that Williams had hoped for since conceiving of *The Rose Tattoo* with her in mind. The Italian star portrayed Lady Torrance in the film that was renamed *The Fugitive Kind* and featured Marlon Brando as Val Xavier. The film had star power enough to merit a pulp release of *Orpheus* featuring its new title.

Nineteen sixty also saw Williams' first full-length Christmas offering to the world: *Period of Adjustment.* The three main scenic elements referred to in the play are the beds (naturally), the couch, and the television across from the couch. In *Period,* Williams addresses a social disease he sees emanating from the tubes in the monstrous box. The plot is simple, especially by the standards of Williams' full-length plays. Ralph Bates is a dissatisfied office worker. He feels enslaved by his boss, who is also his wife's father. Years back, Papa/boss man Mr. McGillicuddy alluded to his own impending demise, making a sideways promise to Ralph that he'd receive the fortune for the dairy empire Mr. Mac had built. He's hung on for lo these many years, however, and now Ralph is at the end of his rope, feeling he's been somehow cheated by his father-in-law's unexpected longevity. He quits work on Christmas morning and has a row with his wife over the ordeal. She has left the house as the play begins, and Ralph has just gotten news that his old war buddy is popping in with his brand-new bride for an impromptu visit. What could go wrong?

What goes wrong is that George, Ralph's buddy, is equally (if not more) unlucky in love on this particular Christmas than Ralph himself. He's barely spoken to his bride since the night before, when they had a failed attempt at consummating their union in a roadside motel. Everything seems to have gone wrong for them, and George decides the best solution is to run off, cool off, and leave his wife, Isabel, in Ralph's care . . . without telling either of them of the plan. Much of the play is composed of Isabel and Ralph getting better acquainted and George and Ralph catching up once George returns.

To this writer's thinking, the play reads a lot like Tennessee Williams putting his own spin on—and considerably elongating—a television sitcom. The stakes are not as dire as with his other writings and there are plenty of lines that beg for a laugh track. It enjoyed a healthy run on Broadway and even garnered a film adaptation released in 1962 featuring Jane Fonda as Isabel Haverstick. If anything stands out in this play, it's that Williams waxes metaphorical on the state of a whole class of people—the sinking middle class.

Ralph Bates is fixated on the television. His buddy from the glory days suggests that beers are being drugged en masse to sedate drinkers, making them more susceptible to the commercials on TV. There's a whole dichotomy between working in a dairy in a dead-end, four-walls existence versus George's plan for himself and his friend: to start a cattle ranch in the frontier country of West Texas and raise animals that would look more historically accurate and regal than those on TV westerns. For all its comedy and low-stakes Christmas foolishness, *Period* seems to issue a dire warning against being too comfortable in Post-War America, lest the human spirit be outshone by the sickly glow of the idiot box.

Points of Interest

- In 1960, *Fugitive Kind* starring Anna Magnani and Marlon Brando is released. It's a film adaptation of *Orpheus Descending*.
- In the same year, *Period of Adjustment* opens on Broadway.
- In 1961, *The Night of the Iguana* opens on Broadway to great renown.

Nineteen sixty-one was a busy year for Williams. It saw two films, a new Broadway opening, and an introduction that would impact the rest of his life. Let's focus on the Broadway opening before circling back around to the rest. Along with *Menagerie, Cat, Streetcar,* and a handful of other "canon" Tennessee Williams plays, *Night of the Iguana* occupies a special place in the pantheon on Williams' dramas. Setting aside that it opened with Bette Davis in one of the primary roles (worth the price of admission for all of the mugging, I'm sure), *Iguana* had much with which to entrance audiences: copious religious imagery, discussion of underwear fetish masturbation, Nazis, and a giant lizard, which—sadly—we never see.

Maxine Faulk owns a rustic hotel in Costa Verde, Mexico, where the Reverend T. Lawrence

Shannon has brought a busload of ladies on a tour. Shannon does not know two things: the rapacious Maxine is recently a widow and has been sating her sexual needs by diddling the young men who work for her, and that Shannon himself has come to this place at the end of the world for some kind of escapist absolution. Defrocked for some time, he's not been a reverend for a while, and the same situation that got his collar snatched seems to pursue him still. Women can't keep their hands off of Shannon, and he is terrible at boundaries. Some of the women who molest the good preacher have been indiscreet, so out of the clergy he was flung, and he's been making a living at giving bus tours while on his cockeyed spirit quest. Whether Shannon wanted the advances or not? Williams seems to leave this intentionally ambiguous.

The battle for Shannon's body becomes a four-way struggle. Maxine offers a warm, carefree possibility for a future if he surrenders to her lazy way of life and her volcanic bed. One of the women on the bus tour is obsessed with him, too, and she's far too young for all that—a situation that has not escaped the watchful eye of her hawk-like lady chaperone. Shannon is trying to keep himself together, lest he shake apart and lose all semblance of self to one of these women. That's when Hannah Jelkes presents herself. A foil to Maxine's burning desire, she's a cool spring of water. Shannon hopes that she can heal his splintered spirit when she presents an image of herself that is all patience and non-judgment. Or, option four, he could just run away elsewhere, prolonging his pain and penance, by choosing not to choose.

The spoiler is that Shannon's problem can't be solved by any of the women, it seems. Even after being tied up and sedated by Hannah, he can't seem to see that his own agency mustn't be dictated by another person (an extremely agnostic notion, seemingly paradoxical for a minister to grasp!). At the play's conclusion, the molten-mouthed matron Maxine stands victorious on her mountaintop stronghold with Shannon as her prize, and the captured stud frees the titular iguana from his captivity. The animal spends much of the play skittering and scratching beneath the boards of the hotel, chained up awaiting its appointment to be served on a plate. Shannon rescues the wild beast in an effort to save someone, himself surrendering.

The character of Shannon, Williams admits, was based loosely on characteristics of his cousin Sidney Lanier, an ex-preacher himself, and another scion of the Tennessee Laniers. Williams shared an apartment in New York with his cousin for a while. The other composite portrait in *Iguana* was Hanna Jelkes's grandfather Nonno, an extremely aged but still active painter, who bore similarities to Williams' grandfather Dakin.

The drama and the performances of the original Broadway production were as delicious to audiences and critics as a fresh-braised iguana filet. Material that would have been too smutty only fifteen years earlier was becoming decent enough to be described and presented for polite audiences in big houses, and Williams succeeded in eroticizing another male body for the gentry.

It seemed that Williams had created a well-understood lexicon for audiences and critics with which to regard his works. The two films released that same year supported this vocabulary. *The Roman Spring of Mrs. Stone* starring Vivien Leigh and Warren Beatty and *Summer and Smoke* starring Geraldine Page rounded out a prolific year for our hero. It's a pity that his momentum, having built to a meteoric pitch for more than a decade, would have to meet the end of so many shooting stars.

SCENIC ROUTE

"The fugitive kind" was a phrase that Williams often revisited throughout his creative career. Several mentions are prominently featured in his plays, poems, and stories. They all amount to those outsiders who can't escape an encroaching, persecuting world that seeks to consume and punish them. It was even the title of an earlier play from the 1930s in Williams' "apprentice" playwright period. The 1937 full-length drama is set in a flophouse in St. Louis on a wintry night (certainly colder than the Delta rainy season leading up to Easter that the film is set against). The vagrants and unfortunates populating the low-rent situation have all brought their own demons to press against the walls from the outside. In *Fugitive Kind,* Williams doesn't achieve a decisively insightful expression of an individual character as he later would in the Blanches, Maggies, and Amandas, but he clearly exhibited a strong grip of greater societal woes facing people who live un-charmed lives on the uncharted fringes of society.

It is certainly curious and *very* "Tennesseean" that for a film, he reworked a play that was the reworking of an earlier play, and the title for the film was a recycled title of a much earlier play. The through lines were, for this particular author, evident and strong through much of his career.

IX

DEAD PLANET, THE MOON

Point of Interest

- According to many, 1961 is approximately when Tennessee Williams suddenly became a no-longer great playwright.

Momentum insists that its object keep moving, or else the momentum has no choice but to diminish. It can stumble to a halt or it can crash. Either of these descriptions could be apt for what happened to Tennessee Williams starting in 1961. To say that his star fizzled, one has to assert that—at least for a time—he became less prolific, less brilliant. That's subjective. It can't be dismissed outright, but I subscribe to a different theory. I think he crashed. So many undeniably devastating events came down on Williams in the early 1960s that one has to consider their collective impact on his work and the subsequent effects on his reputation. But here I go getting ahead of myself, talking about his reputation, when perhaps you don't know.

American wisdom has been for decades that Tennessee Williams was America's greatest playwright *up to a point.* That point for those wise people tends to be *Night of the Iguana.* After that point, learnéd individuals who matriculated in the best programs and bear all the badges and offices of goodly smartness would contend that Williams turned into a drunky-drunk crap monster doomed to churn out hysterical nonsense, and never again to scrape the heights of his own brilliance. They applaud his good works but charitably assign to his later works (post-*Iguana*) the categorization of "lesser Williams," as though he must have hit some existential expiration date, after which his output was uniformly sour.

I would contend that most of those same wizened folk aren't familiar with the plethora of "lesser Williams" that he put out before the 1960s, because we Americans love our boxes and our pert narratives. I instead prefer the narrative that's more complex, shared by readers and theatregoers in other parts of the world. Tennessee Williams was America's greatest playwright. Period. Now, that's subjective, too, sure. You may be able to cite a stronger impact made by O'Neill, Miller, Inge, Hellman, Wilson, and so on. Those are valid arguments. However, if one is to decide on Williams as holding the moniker of AGP, it's unfair to apply the "up to a point" caveat.

Not all of Williams' works were the masterstrokes that *Menagerie, Streetcar,* and *Cat* were, it's true. For better or for worse, the "Big Three" set an Olympus-high bar against which his other works would forever be compared. After all, once you've had the best hamburger, everything else is just a sandwich. There are still some damn good sandwiches to be had, though. That's where the well-known canon or the "Essential Williams" fits in. From there, the "lesser Williams" is perhaps more niche, definitely more obscure, less frequently performed and all that . . . but the stuff is still good, mostly. In many cases, some of Williams' lesser-known works have amassed a cult following, even.

To demystify the baffling notion that Williams abruptly fell off a creative cliff, we must strive to better understand the pressures that led to a stumble that turned into a downhill tumble for the playwright.

In the early 1960s, Williams suffered no small number of deaths of loved ones. Since this is *Tennessee Williams 101,* I haven't gone into detail about every single nerdy famous-faces-of-Mid-Century-America connection Williams had. Suffice to say, he circulated amid the movers, shakers, and significant tastemakers of the day. Starting in the 1960s, I could compile a chronological appendix just composed of the ones who died on him and broke his poet's heart (I won't; that's morbid).

The most significant death was Frank Merlo. With more than thirteen years of shared life between them, Williams and Merlo had drifted apart in the last few years of Merlo's life. Being estranged, it was a staggering blow to Williams to find that Merlo was suffering from advanced lung cancer. In the months leading up to Frank's passing, Williams brought Frank home to care for him as best he could. He saw to it that Frank was provided for, and Frank put up a good front in spite of the fact that Williams was also seeing someone else during the ordeal. Frank cohabited the Key West compound with Frederick Nicklaus, an aspiring poet whom Williams had taken a shining to.

At the age of forty, Frankie, whom Tennessee dubbed his "Little Horse" breathed his last breath, and left Tennessee in the grips of a grieving-guilt not dissimilar to the one he felt when Rose had been lobotomized while he was off and about in the world. The year was 1963. In the same year, Williams' play *The Milk Train Doesn't Stop Here Anymore* flopped on Broadway, closed almost immediately, and was regarded by audiences and critics as a garish misstep.

These two serious blows, along with a handful of other deaths in the space of a couple of years, were underlined by something sinister that had been taking place since 1961. That's the year in which Williams became a patient of Dr. Max Jacobson, infamously known as "Dr. Feelgood." He was not a good doctor.

Alongside other high-profile patients like John F. Kennedy and Judy Garland, Tennessee Williams was subject to quackery that may have felt good in the moment, but was textbook bad medicine. It is well-known that Jacobson used pseudoscience and other questionable methods to treat his unwitting clientele. Such methods included vitamin injections that were not evidence-based in their development (at best) and harmful (at worst). In the guise of treatment for wellbeing, he used rich human subjects as lab rats for his mad science experiments, and Williams was one of them. His treatment also had a more traditionally pharmaceutical lean, though—it wasn't all snake oil.

Regrettably, Dr. Jacobson's dispensation of more traditional prescriptions was especially generous; his discernment with them commensurately lax. Jacobson wrote Williams liberal prescriptions for drugs, which the playwright used ad nauseam. Throughout his hardships in the 1960s, Williams was overmedicated to a dangerous degree. When he somewhat snapped out of it in the 1970s, he'd call the period his "Stoned Age."

His personal struggles throughout this Stoned Age were on display for the world, which had disastrous effects on his reputation and reception as a dramatist. There was a growing fixation with the personal lives of famous people. Whereas before, celebrities were akin to deities and only the most indiscreet characters might come under fire for their lifestyles, the gossip engine was roaring at all hours in the latter half of the twentieth century. A low-tech precursor to the current 24-hour gossip/news/opinion mill, I refer to this as the 12-hour news cycle, and it was brutal for those entertainment personalities who were like ants under the merciless paparazzi's scalding magnifying glass.

Writers were not spared from the critical eye of the rumor-hungry public. Scandals became as well-publicized as the openings of plays or releases of novels. Williams' contemporaries like Vidal and Capote were forearmed with sharp tongues and pens to write off the assaults by those they estimated to be lesser wits. Vidal's self-assuredness made him diamond-hard. Capote, on the other hand, was all made up of knives—he had a remark or one-up for any sling or arrow loosed at him, no matter how outrageous. Meanwhile, there were some satirists and shit-stirrers who relished in the stink eye of the plebeians. Williams was made neither of diamonds, knives, nor was he empowered by the winces.

Williams had bluster to be sure, and when he wrote letters to Windham, Vidal, Capote, and other associates, he had much to say about the "nervous aunties" shrieking *"quelle horreur!"* at witnessing the gay life. In practice, though, he was much more sensitive than the others. He took to heart the reception of critics, the unenthusiastic responses of audiences, the absence of laughter at his jokes. In his weakened state, his personal flaws were brought into stark relief, and the journalists of the day took note—and advantage. Tennessee Williams became known as an eccentric in the 1960s . . . and not the good kind. He was woefully unprepared for the merciless reporting on his every misstep.

Being gay did not do his reputation any favors in the mid-1900s. Homosexual acts were still punished criminally in much of the country, and the stigma ran deep. While Williams hadn't yet publicly discussed his homosexuality, the writing was clearly on the wall for anyone with functioning eyes or ears and a ticket to his plays. Vidal and Capote threw up proverbial middle fingers in cavalier defiance, and Williams . . . well, he did his best to keep a brave face. Being seen as a degenerate by much of his audience did not suit the playwright. His poetic heart yearned for acceptance, and nasty stories about his drugged-up gay exploits did nothing to earn him that.

During this trying time, however, Williams didn't cease writing. No matter how tough it got, Williams kept up his writing efforts. Although the mid-1960s accounts for a considerable gap in primary sources—those are, letters and drafts—compared to any other period in his lifetime, there's still enough evidence to know that the old sport was still hammering away at the veil between human experience and human understanding.

After the disastrous clo'pening of *Milk Train,* thanks in part to a blizzard and scant press due to a strike (a one-two punch than nearly doomed *Menagerie* except for Ashton and Stevens's valiant intervention), Williams and those who still believed in producing his work tried something that had not been tried since José Quintero remounted *Summer and Smoke:* going back to the scene of a disaster. The first *Milk Train* attempt was in January 1963. Almost a year later, it was revived with famous actress Tallulah Bankhead, and the outcome was a little different. The first production ran for two months. The second survived less than a week. The same year, *Night of the Iguana* was adapted for the silver screen to some acclaim, headed up by heartthrob du jour Richard Burton (famous for his tumultuous marriage to Elizabeth Taylor), co-starring Ava Gardner (famous for having been married to Frank Sinatra) and Deborah Kerr (famous for being Deborah Kerr).

With the twin failures of *Milk Train* and the success of *Iguana,* Williams had kept his head just high enough above water (spilt milk?) to move forward with a new-old play called *The Eccentricities of a Nightingale.* It was a reworking of *Summer and Smoke* wherein he tightened and reimagined some symbols and exchanges—probably the most significant among the changes was the exorcising of the problematic portrayal of Mexican characters (A word of caution: if you find yourself doing *Summer and Smoke,* handle those roles with care, lest you find yourself making minstrels of a marginal group—never a good thing). For all the work put into the play, it was published but not produced.

Points of Interest

- In 1961, Williams becomes a patient of Dr. Max Jacobson, alias "Dr. Feelgood."
- In 1963, Frank Merlo dies at 40 from lung cancer.
- In 1963, *The Milk Train Doesn't Stop Here Anymore* runs on Broadway for a disastrously short run of two months. In the following year, it is revived and runs less than a week.
- Throughout the 1960s and '70s, Williams and other notable writers become celebrities and are subjected to the scrutiny of the press and public in a new and intense way.

During this challenging period, Williams was exercising more unusual conventions as a playwright. Perhaps inspired by the surreal sensations of being overmedicated, his experimental urges were coming more into focus in his writing. While he'd always been an experimentalist, it had not been since *Camino Real* that he attempted to push forth a "weird play" for public consumption.

A bizarre and delightful offering for the '60s was a double bill entitled *Slapstick Tragedy.* The title should have been a clear enough indicator that the style would be intentionally disjointed, but audiences who came expecting either a slapstick comedy or a high tragedy (or the traditional Deep South Tennessee Williams fare) were not pleased. Seven shows into its run, much like *Milk Train* redux, *Slapstick Tragedy* tragically closed.

Critics and audiences simply didn't know what to make of the evening composed of two long one-act plays. While they're admittedly bizarre, they have their merits. Sadly, those merits got lost in 1966 because the presentation was too far out. Like with *Camino,* viewers didn't have enough common vocabulary to safely latch onto the surreal experience, and like with *Camino,* I'll do my best to unpack what unfolded onstage. Fortunately, these plays are a *little* more linear in the traditional sense.

The evening began with *The Gnädiges Fräulein.* If the title weren't alienating enough, the material soon would be. At curtain, a society writer named Polly is being assaulted by menacing, carnivorous birds as she approaches a rooming house named the Big Dormitory. For a lover of Williams, the first scenario and the semantics of it are delightfully riddled with Easter eggs. The carnivorous birds are a call back to *Suddenly Last Summer,* as is the naming of a hotel for adults called a dormitory— it hearkens to Catharine recalling the notion that all of humanity is a kindergarten classroom. Polly introduces the tone of the play by presenting herself as a bastion of biased reporting. She's harassed by a flock of beasts hungry for anything that's thrown to them. She is an overt representation of the press and Williams' attitude toward them at the time— an unflattering portrayal to be sure.

Once Polly evades the fictional cocalooney birds, she arrives at the Big Dormitory to meet Molly, the landlady. Whereas Polly represents the press, Molly and her Big Dormitory represent producers and theatres. It's no wonder that when Polly calls on her, Molly is mopping up blood from last night's blunder. The front porch—a stage of sorts—is drenched in the genetic material of a once-famous entertainer named the Gnädiges Fräulein ("Gracious" or "Kind Lady," more or less). Molly regales Polly with the fine points of the Big Dormitory, hoping to get a feature in Polly's rag. Polly is skeptical to the point of bitchiness, and the two grapple verbally until the cocalooney bird descends on them both to remind them that supper has to be served to the ravenous masses sooner or later.

When we finally meet the Fräulein, she's a pitiful sight. Her eye was gouged out in an expedition into the realm of the cocalooney birds, but she simply can't stop trying to work out her tired old act and scrape together a living. She represents the artist who places their work on the stage: if comparing to Williams, the writer. In the Fräulein, Williams showed a beaten down, half-blind (as he had been for some parts of his life) has-been who can't give up the ghost. She's preyed upon by the landlord (producer), the society columnist (gossipy press), and even the birds (the audience). In a final confrontation, she loses her other eye and wanders blind onto the stage to try and cook a meal that is stolen from her without her knowledge. Even after all the horror, she can't give up the desire to try.

It would have been a heartbreaking portrayal if the audience and critics had not been so flabbergasted by it. In fact, I would guess that

Fräulein was so shocking that folks forgot about the second half of the double bill, which was much more straightforward: *The Mutilated.*

The Mutilated is not what one would expect to be the title of a Christmas musical, but that's essentially what it was. The scenes are punctuated by Christmas carols with lyrics by Williams himself. In the first lines of a haunting Chrismas carol as the curtain rises, the show announces itself to be about "the strange, the crazed, the queer"—those fugitive kind that Williams so often returned to.

The action of *The Mutilated* follows two old friends-turned-enemies one Christmas Eve in the French Quarter of New Orleans. Celeste has just been released from jail and is starving. Setting hunger aside, she's really hankering for a drink. She heads to her ex-friend Trinket's hotel room to find that she's still on her old pal's naughty list. Trinket is an oil heiress with a past. She stays in a fleabag hotel on Rampart Street to isolate herself from humiliation about her past indiscretions and to prevent anyone from learning that she is "mutilated." Her mutilation a mastectomy scar, having survived a battle with cancer. Celeste is her only friend who knows about Trinket's situation, and has threatened Trinket with exposing it to others.

Over the course of that Christmas Eve, Trinket attempts to avoid Celeste while hunting a man to bring home to assuage her loneliness. Celeste, on the other hand, sets out to stalk and pester Trinket—in part to get revenge, in part to assuage her own loneliness. Trinket eventually scores a drunken sailor and evades Celeste. The next morning, Trinket and Celeste reconcile their differences and avoid the doom that befalls lost souls in the winter of cities. They are terribly drunk.

The plays are hilarious if executed comedically. The audiences in 1966 were not laughing, though.

Slapstick Tragedy became another painful flop on the quickly growing pile. Williams had already been working on another unusual play in a meta-theatrical vein, which would be the next to be produced. *The Two-Character Play* is about two actors on a stage preparing for a play—or are they?—and psychologically unravelling as they do so. This piece will resurface again more than once, so here I'll just establish that it opened in London in 1967, and that Williams was dissatisfied with how it turned out. He was coming to terms with the creative drag his physical, mental, and pharmacological states were putting on him in the years following Frank's death. So, he went back to work on it and spent several years drafting and revising it. Meanwhile he was steadily crafting something in more familiar territory—the Delta.

While *Two-Character* struggled abroad, stateside Williams was piecing together a Southern thriller called *Kingdom of Earth.* Years before, Williams devised a sultry short story with plenty of erotic imagery and a few touches of delightful blasphemy with the same title. Next, Williams converted it into a short play, and the characters began to take more definite shape. Finally, he expanded it into a full-length play that would be completed in 1968 that had all the trappings of a Southern *Psycho* story that would make Alfred Hitchcock proud.

It is a dark and stormy winter night when Lot Ravenstock brings home his blushing, effusive bride, Myrtle Kane. He has driven her down from Memphis where they met the day before (not unlike in *Period of Adjustment*). They arrive at the dilapidated Delta farmhouse of Lot's family on the eve of what could be a true disaster. It's been raining for an interminable time, and the water is about to overtop the levees. If that happens, everything will be lost, including the lives of those caught in the flood. Myrtle learns this news at the same time as the audience; the revelation causing her great distress. She is also concerned that Lot's demeanor is odd, grumbly, and aloof. Further, he appears to be obsessed with his dead mother.

Myrtle, having been an opportunist, didn't think twice before marrying Lot on television (yes, a game-show marriage). She didn't consider that he was pale, coughed a lot, and had conspicuously bleached hair. None of these red flags deterred Myrtle from latching onto a nice young man who had no second thoughts about marrying a complete stranger. Williams' characters don't always make sound decisions, and that's what we love about them.

There's one more surprise waiting for Myrtle behind door number one. Lot has a brother, referred to only as Chicken. He is a swarthy, menacing, salt-of-the-earth farmhand bastard. No, really. He's the bastard brother of Lot. They seem to hate each other, but there's a humming tension that surges between the brothers and Myrtle. She slowly comes to terms with the fact that she's married a man wracked with tuberculosis and who has dragged Myrtle into mortal danger. To make matters worse, she's hungry. After retiring to Lot's mother's old room where Lot intends for them to spend their married nights, Myrtle must descend the steps to the kitchen to face Chicken and ask for some food.

What ensues is a tug-of-war up and down the stairs, each time revealing greater character development of one of the players in the game. Eventually Myrtle surrenders to Chicken, Chicken saves Myrtle from the flood waters, and Lot staggers downstairs dressed in his dead mother's clothing, seemingly possessed by her, moments before drowning in the deluge.

In 1968, *Kingdom* opened on Broadway under the title *The Seven Descents of Myrtle* (because that rolls off the tongue . . .). The name change was at the suggestion of the producer and Broadway heavyweight David Merrick. The seven descents refer to the original six times Myrtle goes down the stairs, and the final time when she performs oral sex on Chicken. By the time the show opened, it seems that some of the descents had been cut, making the name all the more mystifying. The show received some applause and critics were marginally pleased that Williams had returned to the Delta setting. It was not a blockbuster, though, and failed to catapult Williams back into the good graces of reviewers and theatregoers.

He simply couldn't get the mojo back. He knew that he wasn't doing his greatest work, and spent much of his time intoxicated or narcotized under drugs. He drank as profusely as he wrote, and his friends pitied him if they were near enough to him to do so. Many of his friends had been alienated or died. Williams was seriously depressed. He was working through it, but the exit ladder atop his creative tunnel seemed always just out of reach.

Williams' struggles in the 1960s didn't go unnoticed by his family. His younger brother, Dakin, was concerned about how troubled his brother was, and he took steps to correct it. One step was to get Tennessee some God. In 1969, Dakin convinced Tennessee to convert to Roman Catholicism, but that was a farcical notion that didn't ultimately stick. More than anything, it seems to have given Dakin something to be proud of. In the same year, Dakin had Tennessee committed for psychiatric care at Barnes Hospital in St. Louis for three months. This stay allowed Tennessee to level off and dry out, presenting a sort of reset from his previous course of medication, which had been too much and inconsistently administered. Dakin struck out on the Church, but he at least helped derail Dr. Feelgood's bullet train to certain ruin for Tennessee. Dakin and the staff of the hospital omitted the truth that, after a point, Williams could have checked himself out of his own free will. Once Williams later learned of this, he never forgave Dakin for the equivocation, and punished him with his final will and testament, leaving Dakin a pittance when compared to other beneficiaries. Regardless of the trick that was played on him, he was presented with a new lease on a healthier life—perhaps his life was even saved.

But was he already too ruined? Had America's greatest playwright become an asset so toxic he wasn't worth investing in? Vidal thought not. In 1970, he worked to adapt *Kingdom/Seven Descents* into a film under yet *another* title, *The Last of the Mobile Hot Shots* (a direct reference to Myrtle's situation as the only surviving member of her troupe of lady entertainers). Laughlin also refused to abandon Williams. New Directions published *Dragon Country,* a substantial collection of strong one-act plays. There were still those who had faith in Old Tennessee. Would they be enough to support his climb out of the trench he'd nearly been buried in? And what of the ever-stalwart Audrey Wood, and Williams' other angels?

Points of Interest

- In 1966, *Slapstick Tragedy* opens on Broadway featuring two long one-act plays, *The Gnädiges Fräulein* and *The Mutilated.*
- *The Two-Character Play* opens in England in 1967 and is published.
- In 1968, *The Seven Descents of Myrtle,* also known as *Kingdom of Earth* opens on Broadway.
- In 1969, Dakin Williams has his brother, Tennessee, committed to Barnes Hospital for psychiatric care for three months.

X

ON A CLIFF AT THE EDGE OF THE WORLD

Tennessee Williams had a recurring setting in his plays: places at the edge of the world. At least the solid world. He was interested in stories that take place on coasts and frontiers. Even New Orleans seems to be on the verge of dissolving into its surrounding brackish waters and wilderness when he described the city in *Streetcar* and *Suddenly Last Summer.* Characters who are transient flit in and out of the "safe" world. Tom Wingfield recedes into the dark back corners of the movies, dreaming of departing for far-off seas, only coming back home out of begrudging duty in *The Glass Menagerie.* The dragon country that lays outside the borders of the small towns in *Orpheus Descending* and the deep drop-off into nothingness of *Night of the Iguana* are equally hostile and enticing. In *Milk Train,* the bottom of the cliff that Sissy Goforth nests atop features an out-of-the-way cottage called the "oubliette," from the French "oublier," meaning "to forget."

To be forgotten or to fade into obscurity is something prominent in much of Williams' body of work. In the 1970s, Williams realized that he had spent nearly an entire decade hovering on the precipice of disaster, but by the grace of God and intrepid friends, he was prevented from utter obliteration. If he had died during his "Stoned Age," tabloids and even the legitimate newspapers would have had no choice but to report the failing playwright of waning talent had overdosed or drunk himself to death—a fitting end to a talent wasted. He had been dangling in danger he didn't fully grasp, distracted as he was wrestling with an ever-worsening malaise.

Almost concurrently with Dakin's committing Tennessee for care, *In the Bar of a Tokyo Hotel* was playing for a few weeks Off-Broadway. The run was a footnote in Williams' theatrical career and the play only gets produced every so often to this day, but it's a startling reflection of what Williams was likely going through at the time he was finishing it and seeing it staged. The play takes place, as the title states, in the bar of a hotel in Tokyo. There is only one character native to Japan: the Barman. The central character is an American woman named Miriam, who is spending all day in the bar of the hotel while her husband, Mark, a famous artist, is having a nervous breakdown upstairs. He is trying to approach a new form of creation. He thinks he's on the verge of making the first true discovery of color. Miriam thinks it's a crock of shit. Secretly, she wishes he would return to a more consumer-friendly medium and execution, but she does not dare tell him what to do. Instead, she drinks. She hides. She hits on the steely bartender.

Eventually, Mark makes his way downstairs and Miriam expresses her dissatisfaction with their situation. She has accompanied him to a foreign country where she knows almost no one and has been made to endure his mad ramblings and chaotic process. She's at the end of the world with him and terrified that he's going to pull her into the abyss. She makes a panicked plea to Mark's art dealer Leonard, who appears in the second half of the play. Neither Miriam nor Leonard is able to come up with an adequate solution for Mark's unraveling of mind and spirit, so his heart gives out, he dies, and Miriam ends the play more lost than she began.

The art Mark is producing is described as being splattered and the phrase "spray gun" is bandied about, giving sure allusion to Jackson Pollock, the legendary painter of the mid-twentieth century. Pollock died only a few years before Williams completed *Tokyo Hotel,* and Williams was an admirer of the painter. There's no doubt that he related to the meteoric rise of Pollock in the art world and the pressure to continue turning out sublime pieces.

An aesthetic **detour to Japan:** aside from Pollock's paintings, an art form that inspired parts of *Tokyo Hotel* was Noh Theatre, a cultural convention in Japan. Williams had visited Japan a couple of times after having met Yukio Mishima, the Japanese writer and political activist. Their first encounter, or so it is told, was cruising the streets of Manhattan, but within only a few days they met in a professional setting— perhaps that's when they learned each other's names. Williams was captivated by Mishima's aesthetic and the Japanese theatrical methods. He borrowed elements from Noh and Kabuki and implemented them in a few plays, never with much fidelity. Perhaps the reasons his use of Japanese conventions was troubled is that he had an incomplete understanding of the context, purpose, and cultural framework in which they were based. Without a holistic understanding of the art form, it broached on appropriation or homage more than thoughtful, complete execution. While not present in *Tokyo Hotel,* one trapping that he fancied from Japanese theatre was the announcement of the most climactic moment of the plot action at the start of the play. We can now merge back into the greater narrative, concluding this Eastern **detour.**

The 1970s gave Williams a second chance to pick up his life and his career, and he took it. While he never kicked his use of Seconal, an addictive barbiturate, most of Dr. Jacobson's course of treatment was terminated. Williams also indicated in letters, and I've learned anecdotally, that he no longer had the constitution to handle the volume of alcohol he had previously been able to consume. Williams continued writing daily, having alleviated much of the queasy drug haze he spent the 1960s in. His plays became more coherent and linear, for the most part. He still experimented with style and unusual material, but the audience in the '70s was becoming increasingly friendly with material that was less traditional and more symbolic and expressive—thanks in part to a new generation of marginalized artists rising to prominence.

Williams saw an enemy to his growth potential in the unlikeliest of places, though. Over the course of the 1960s, Williams soured on Audrey Wood. The agent who in many instances set him up for his initial and successive successes seemed to him now an adversary. In letters he would often suggest she was out to get him, or that she didn't support his efforts any longer. It was not the case, but his paranoia had gotten the better of him.

In 1971, during the rehearsals for the Chicago tryout of *The Two-Character Play,* Williams broke off with Wood for good, and they never exchanged words again. Behind the scenes, Audrey would still care for Williams' affairs at the agency, but her machinations were unknown to him. The work Williams did in the 1970s would make any representative's job unpredictable, as he presented diverse offerings in various styles.

Commensurately with the dissimilar styles and topics he covered in the '70s, so too was the decade a mixed bag when it came to how Williams' plays were received. In 1972, *Small Craft Warnings* could be considered to have been a success. It ran for half a year. Noteworthy about this production are a few casting decisions. It featured Candy Darling, an out transgender artist in the role of Violet, and Tennessee Williams himself even graced the stage in the role of Doc. Williams' turn onstage was a publicity stunt, for sure, but Williams reflected on his time onstage fondly. His next play, *Out Cry,* however, was a flop whose run lasted barely more than seven days. It was a reworking of *The Two-Character Play* with considerably more fine-tuned dialogue but essentially the same perplexing premise.

The plot in *Out Cry* is challenging to follow because of the central conceit of the play itself. It comes off like Williams was channelling Luigi Pirandello's *Six Characters in Search of an Author.* Williams penned a play within a play scenario with only two characters. Clare and Felice are sister and brother, both nervous and psychically wounded. They spend much of the play striving not to appear as unhinged as they obviously are. Their conflict is sometimes assisted, sometimes hindered by their given circumstance: they're supposed to be doing a play. Right now. They're bewildered because they've set foot onstage in an unknown place, having been abandoned by their acting troupe (probably because they're grating and unhinged), with the set half-erected, bizarre pieces that do not belong in their show, and an ominous prop: a handgun.

Clare and Felice are disturbed by the suicide of their parents, but the audience can't be sure if it's a real death or a fictional one, as the lines between play and play-within-play risk coming across blurry. They untangle their emotions and try to make sense of the situation for the audience (which may or may not be imaginary, as well), until they are finally faced with an unwritten scene to which they're inexorably drawn: to pull the trigger or not, and on whom?

Out Cry (1973) and its earlier and later iterations, both called *The Two-Character Play* (1967 and 1976) are straight character development behind a facade of rising action. The emotional heights of the story account for the real payoff for the viewer. The characters are frantic, the stakes are high, and the situation is occasionally confusing and hard to relate to. All of these challenges indicate why Williams saw reason to put additional care into the text before it was ultimately published in its final form a few years after the Broadway disaster.

A play that can be compared and contrasted with *Out Cry* is *Small Craft Warnings*. In *Small Craft,* very little happens as plot goes. It's like *Out Cry* in that way. What separates them most crucially is that the situation and characters in *Small Craft* are supremely relatable and notably diverse (well, as diverse as a group of white actors on Broadway could have looked in the '70s—*socioeconomically* diverse, I suppose I should say). The setting of *Small*

Craft is Monk's Bar, a seaside dive on a cliffside in Southern California on a particularly foggy night in which there is in place—you guessed it—a small craft warning. For those of you not of the nautical persuasion, this sort of advisory warns smaller waterborne vessels to exercise caution as visibility is low due to fog or some other meteorological impediment. The metaphor Williams chose to apply here is that singular, lost individuals floating about in life must be careful so as not to crash or drift out beyond their ability to return.

Monk has a crew of regulars. They drift in throughout the play and are joined by a pair of unusual additions. At the start, Monk is accompanied by Doc, a local doctor who has lost his license for practicing while drunk, and Bill, a local rake and overall nearly worthless hunk of man-meat. His entire value is summed up in his meat. His penis is epic in size, making him a hot commodity for horny locals and transients. Imagine if all of Val Xavier or John Buchanan's best assets and been traded in for their genitals, and you have Bill. Then there is Violet, a dreamy youngish woman resigned to a life of degenerate poverty because she has either no self-worth or advanced neurosyphilis (this is my estimation based on her habits and some textual clues, but it's never confirmed . . . so we'll call her "dreamy"). Violet hangs out in the bar because she has no place to go other than a nasty apartment, and nothing to eat that isn't given to her. She's managed to snag a sad-sack of a boyfriend in Steve, who eventually ambles into the bar, and he's reliable for getting her a bite to eat every now and then at the nearby Burger King.

The most climactic moment onstage is in the first twenty minutes, when Leona busts into the bar with a bug in her bonnet looking for Bill, her beau. Leona was busy making dinner for the two of them when she looked up to see Bill had abandoned her to go to the bar. She left her trailer behind to come round up her wandering stud. After tearing him a new one with some fantastic rants, Leona realizes that Violet has been giving Bill a hand job under the table, and Leona waylays the poor creature. The fight is broken up and Leona begins a string of monologues dressing down the various patrons at the bar.

Leona is eventually interrupted by Quentin, an effete screenwriter who comes in for shelter from the dangerous driving conditions. In tow is Bobby, a young man who Quentin expected to be a sex worker only to find out that he's a sweet, sexually liberated youth, which makes Quentin edgy. Quentin ditches the boy and then the boy cuts out on his own, bicycling into the night. The regulars are left behind, all except Doc, who is called to deliver a baby, which he desperately shouldn't be doing in his inebriated state.

The group quarrels amongst itself a little more until Doc returns with terrible news. The night fizzles to a hopeless-for-some, hopeful-for-others conclusion. Violet manages to get in a little more under-the-table action before finally being admitted to Monk's upstairs apartment out of pity. What makes the play so touching is a holdover from its earlier incarnation, a short play called *Confessional*: monologues to the audience. Each character in the play at some point breaks from the action of the play and directly addresses the viewer. It's a risk Williams took to include direct address, but it pays off by enhancing the intimacy and the understanding of the characters. Being that each character receives a monologue moment and that it's introduced early enough in the play, it doesn't seem jarring or experimental—it seems just right.

Add to this that the situation is so commonplace and the characters are fleshed out not just by their monologues but also by the simplicity of their archetypes—a bartender, hairdresser, fry cook, floozy, doctor, vagrant youth, and others—*Small Craft* was a play for the audience to absolve the characters of the foibles that they judge themselves for. In *Small Craft,* there's just as much carnage as *Streetcar,* and at the end you get a similar payoff: you understand the people around you more deeply and forgive yourself your trespasses. Bill cheats, Leona lashes out, Violet drifts about like a diseased waterlily, and Doc is confronted with the death of a mother and child in tandem—but no character is left with the mark of unpardonable wickedness. In that signature Tennessee Williams way, to paraphrase Blanche in *Streetcar,* cruelty is the only inexcusable trait. To Williams, any other foible was worthy of grace. *Small Craft* is an exoneration for the variegated, wretched Fugitive Kind.

Points of Interest

- In 1969, *In the Bar of a Tokyo Hotel* has a short run Off-Broadway.
- In 1972, *Small Craft Warnings* enjoys a healthy 6-month run in New York. It features cast members Candy Darling and Tennessee Williams during its run.
- *Out Cry* flops on Broadway in 1973.
- Williams' *Memoirs* is published, replete with personal and professional tales of success and woe in 1975.
- In 1976, three plays open: *This Is (An Entertainment)* in San Francisco, *The Red Devil Battery Sign* in

Boston, and *The Eccentricities of a Nightingale* in New York.

Another 1970s play bound for Broadway didn't even survive its out-of-town tryout. In 1976, *The Red Devil Battery Sign,* much like *Battle of Angels* before it, was sent to hell in Boston. In the same year that *Eccentricities of a Nightingale* finally had a life onstage, only to close on Broadway directly after opening. Nineteen seventy-three was a rough year for new plays by Mr. Williams. However, he was beginning to come around to a very curious notion: what if a play doesn't have to go to Broadway?

It had been years since Williams had a new play that ran its entire course in a smaller market (by small, meaning not in London or New York . . . you know, the two most massive English-speaking markets). Margo Jones, in his more obscure years, had seen to it that a few of Williams' plays were produced in California. Ever his champion, she saw no fault in a solid regional production. It seemed novel, I suppose, after his receiving a plethora of Drama Critics' Circle Awards and a pair of Pulitzers, to return to the dimmer lights cast by marquees away from the Great White Way.

Way out west in San Francisco, American Conservatory Theatre staged Tennessee Williams' saucy and riotous new play *This Is (An Entertainment).* In the safety of a market not shackled to the unforgiving beast of Broadway, it was able to open without fear of immediately closing. The limited run might have taken off some of the sting that came with a show that had been planted on Broadway, but perhaps had never been meant for that ecosystem. In 1978, two years after *This Is,* a stage version of *Baby Doll* named *Tiger Tail* opened in Atlanta, where after Williams was able to revise it based on what he felt it needed, then it opened again in Florida. Both productions completed their runs. Who could say if it could have played so robustly in a more carnivorous market?

The two scheduled short runs formed parentheses around another spectacular failure on Broadway with *Vieux Carré*. Playing only five days, the play could have been dubbed a sequel to *The Glass Menagerie*. Like *Menagerie,* it features a narrator who is personally involved in the action. This time, he's called The Writer (another TW anagram like Tom Wingfield). The story takes place in the French Quarter (colloquially known in pidgin French as the "VOO kuh-RAY") in the winter of 1938-39. What's special about *Vieux Carré* when placed against *Menagerie* is that it becomes considerably more autobiographical. The characters are still composites of real-life people; don't get me wrong. For example, Mrs. Wire, the overbearing landlord *did* live on the same block as the house Williams stayed in during the winter of '38-'39, but his landlord who fit the bill was named Mrs. Anderson. *Vieux Carré* also featured dialogue and scenarios from a handful of one-act plays such as an exchange about vermin from *The Lady of Larkspur Lotion.*

Other characters fill the rooms of Mrs. Wire's place, such as an aspiring fashion designer dying of cancer, shacked up with a strip-joint barker who's strung out on heroin. There's a pair of starving crones who go dumpster diving wearing the trappings of their glory days, unable to admit they're dirt poor. The landlady haunts the halls nightly with a flashlight, sometimes ensuring there are no unregistered guests, other times in a daze of dementia looking for her missing son. Then there's Nightingale, a painter from a prominent family who has escaped Baton Rouge to live his queer life in the debauched French Quarter only to die of tuberculosis at the conclusion of the play. Whether these were all characters Williams knew in the time frame in which the play takes place, we will surely never know for certain. Maybe they were folks he encountered all around the Quarter, or the world. Either way, *Vieux Carré* stands as one of Williams' two most autobiographical plays— right down to the man from Florida that The Writer skedaddles with by going out West just before the curtain falls.

Williams tips his hand in this play, when he has The Writer admit that "Writers are shameless spies." The retrospective in *Vieux Carré* is more tempered than the one in *Menagerie,* too. It is not as focused on one set of characters. Instead, it focuses on the entire rooming house brimming with the Fugitive Kind. For being so fixated on Williams' personal life details, one would expect audiences to flock to *Vieux Carré.* That was not the case in 1977. But then again, the general audience was not the Easter-egg hunting Williams nerds that we have grown to be!

A few milestones allowed Williams to reclaim the discussion around his personal life, and ignited a more considerate conversation about his career and reputation. The first moment was in 1970, when on David Frost's talk show, Williams candidly spoke about his homosexuality—fresh out of the booby hatch in St. Louis and visibly disheveled, indicating he was not situated firmly on the wagon. The can of worms that was opened was as liberating as it was dangerous. Gone were the days that Williams' sexuality could be a vulnerability, since he reclaimed it on TV, but those close-minded folks who saw him as a reprobate before had fresh, confirmed ammunition moving forward. The second milestone was an interview in *Playboy* magazine.

The *Playboy* interview with C. Robert Jennings ruffled a whole aviary's worth of feathers. Not only did Williams open up about his nonstarter relationships with women, but he used the patently heterosexual and patriarchal platform to regale readers with his gay proclivities and preferences. Less lascivious but more in-depth was one of the longest uninterrupted portions of the interview, dedicated to Williams tenderly explaining his love and history with Frank. He opened up on topics of addiction, critics, and death—heavy fare for a magazine commonly considered dirt, especially at the time.

The third moment in which our hero reclaimed the debate over his soul was in 1975, when his *Memoirs* published. While *Memoirs* has a few time-and-place inconsistencies with what we know about Williams the historical person, Williams the mythic character came into sharp focus with the book's release. It was popular because he talked about the plays that made him famous, of course. It was also popular because of the salacious details of his romantic and personal life. In the years following the Frost interview, Williams spoke unapologetically about his sexuality and how it did—and when he felt it didn't—inform his work. In the 1970s, his gay characters began being portrayed as out characters, rather than closeted or coded.

Compared to characters like *Streetcar*'s Allan Grey and *Cat*'s Skipper, the gay characters were out onstage, rather than ghosts that haunted the men and women in front of the audience. Particularly in Williams' one-act plays, the gay characters take the forestage. Many of these wouldn't be discovered or produced for some decades, but we've got plenty of time to discuss that. What was groundbreaking was for America's greatest playwright (even if he was considered defunct at the time) to present characters like The Writer and Nightingale in *Vieux Carré* and Quentin and Bobby in *Small Craft Warnings* without shrouding their gayness. While he made a historical splash with his out, up-front gay characters, it was not enough to tread water at the box office. With the exception of *Small Craft*'s marginal success, thanks in part to the idea of seeing the famous writer treading the boards, the 1970s was a decade of dignified flops.

Flops or no flops, Williams' ability to pick himself up off the pavement and reconstitute himself as an elder statesman of the American Theatre was impressive. It did not escape the attention of his contemporaries and admirers, and they rewarded it with a parade of incredible honors through the 1970s. It began in 1969 with his receipt of a doctorate of humanities awarded to him by the University of Missouri and a Gold Medal for Drama from the American Academy of Arts and Letters, who would induct him as a member in 1976. In '72, he was awarded two more honorary degrees: one from the University of Hartford and one from Purdue University. The National Arts Club bestowed him with a Medal of Honor for Literature in 1975. The Cannes Film Festival honored Williams with the role of Jury President in 1976. He was awarded with a Kennedy Centers Honors medal by President Jimmy Carter in 1979, and the next year he encountered the president again when he was awarded the Presidential Medal of Freedom in 1980.

The argument over Williams' artistic promise was still being hashed out on Broadway, regardless of what amazing accolades he had collected in the 1970s. He could not separate himself from the desire to be successful in those hallowed auditoriums. They had become homes to which he yearned to return. He associated Broadway with legitimacy, and felt his reputation could be redeemed if he had one more successful go at it. So much was he like one of his own characters: hung up on reputation, desperately seeking to return to a nostalgic idyll, being driven by a need that ran him ragged and ultimately might destroy him. The 1980s would reintroduce him to Broadway, but he would also no longer oppose sending his new, more experimental, and personal work to out-of-town cradles for careful development.

Points of Interest

- From the late 1960s through the early 1980s, Tennessee Williams receives several honors from various national groups concerned with the arts and humanities.
- In 1977, *Vieux Carré* opens on Broadway and closes shortly thereafter.
- In 1978, a stage version of *Baby Doll* titled *Tiger Tail* opens in Atlanta, Georgia.
- In 1979, *A Lovely Sunday for Creve Couer,* set in St. Louis, opens in New York and enjoyed a slightly longer run—one month.

THE SCENIC ROUTE

Returning to Williams' fascination with Japanese elements:

At the beginnings of two plays, *The Milk Train Doesn't Stop Here Anymore* and *The Day on Which a Man Dies,* a character not central to the action proclaims to the audience that the most central character will die at the play's conclusion. This may seem confounding to an audience member who wanted to find out what's next, then next, then next, until the end. Instead, what this tradition forces the audience to do is to forget the idea of linear, action-based plot in favor of seeing how the characters grapple with the inevitability. The dramatic irony also allows the audience to mindfully step back from its instinct to want to discover the end, and instead focus on motive, intention, coping, and so on. *Day on Which* never rose to the prominence of *Milk Train* (maybe "infamy" is a better word?), but as far as we can tell, today's audience is probably more on board with the idea of being told what happens at the end of a story at its beginning. TV shows and movies do it all the time, but it was still a novel, if not unwelcome, concept in the 1960s. Unlike the character named Man in *Day on Which* or Sissy in *Milk Train,* Williams' fate was not predetermined.

XI

FANTASIA

A Lovely Sunday for Creve Couer was Williams'
penultimate realistic full-length play. I make
that statement recognizing I'm including a lot of
qualifiers. It's not his last, and not even his second
to last *play,* or his second to last *full-length* play
(meaning over 90 minutes, if you're wondering
what my benchmark is). I say this because Mr.
Williams was about damn tired of doing plays that
existed in the conventional mode. From his very
beginning, it was never his medium of choice. His
production note in *The Glass Menagerie* way back
in 1943 shows his Expressionist leanings, and to
look at some of the plays published posthumously,
one will recognize he was writing unusual, unique,
and downright strange plays from as early as the
1930s. He even named one short play *The Strange
Play,* and it takes place in a French Quarter
courtyard in about twenty-five minutes, but in
it we see the entire life pass of a woman named
Isabel—complete with her adult son coming back

from fighting in outer space. *A Lovely Sunday for Creve Couer* was no space odyssey.

Creve Couer has three major things going for it: the name is poignant and punny since it translates to "A Lovely Sunday for Heartbreak" (Creve Couer is the name of a park in St. Louis), it has some funny zingers, and it has some fabulous lesbian undertones. I place its daringness in a category alongside *Period of Adjustment,* however, in that it covers little new ground and that its plot is contained to the continuous time and single room in which it takes place—a sort of "Cat on a Mild Tin Roof." It follows the story of a pair of roommates Bodey and Dorothea (a name repeated from *Period*) on a day when they've decided to go to the park. Bodey is trying to set Dorothea up with her brother to ensure she's part of the family forevermore, as Bodey is suggestively romantically inclined toward Dorothea. Enter a slightly less dowdy young woman come to call on Dorothea. Her name is Helena, and she's got plans to scoop Dorothea up and steal her away from the cramped home she keeps with Bodey and settle her friend into a nicer, newer, bigger apartment in a better part of town. The race is on for Bodey to get Dorothea out the door and paired up with her brother, Buddy. Yes, their names are Bodey and Buddy. As Williams goes, it's a chuckle-fest for sure, but as with *Period* it lacks the devastating catharsis present in most of Williams' plays.

Perhaps Williams' *couer* wasn't as invested. He only wrote one more "realistic" play called *A House Not Meant to Stand,* and even that one had surreal underpinnings. Instead, he was busying himself with a handful of more fantastical experiments from 1979 to 1981, all with different flavors: *Will Mr. Merriwether Return from Memphis?; Something*

Cloudy, Something Clear; and *Kirche, Küche, Kinder.*
First came *Kirche, Küche, Kinder,* which translated from German is "church, kitchen, children." It's arranged in the exact reverse order of the actual German saying "kinder, küche, kirche." It was subtitled *An Outrage for the Stage,* and took irreverence to new heights. The church folk are monstrous; the women are aggressively disobedient; and the children are wild, sexualized adults. It reads like a magnificent puppet show camping everything that is supposed to be held in high esteem. Mr. Williams was finished playing nice when it came to plays for general consumption. The production was an experimental workshop held at the Jean Cocteau Repertory Theatre in downtown Manhattan (Where I held my first New York theatre job house managing! Small world.). Of course it didn't grow a second life, but at the very least it began developing a taste for the Williams brand of outrageousness during his lifetime.

The following year saw Williams allowing his work to be crafted outside of the glaring white-hot Broadway glow once more with *Will Mr. Merriwether Return from Memphis?* It debuted in Key West at the performing arts theatre named for Tennessee Williams. It has a massive cast of colorful characters, demands a cakewalk, probably flying elements, and extreme suspension of disbelief. If I had to boil it down to something readily understandable, I would simply say that it's what happens when the wild and weird characters trapped in Williams' small-town Southern settings collide, and the town adapts to them instead of the other way around. *Merriwether* was another limited out-of-town engagement that might (probably for certain) never have happened on Broadway in the early '80s. While Williams was enjoying creative forays into fantasy, one other beautiful dream came to an end.

In 1980, Williams' last true matron of might departed. On June 1, at age 95, Edwina Dakin Williams passed on, leaving Williams with only two leading ladies left: Rose and Maria . . . But you haven't heard of Maria. That's for another chapter.

Let me tell you: there's nothing like the death of a mother to make you reflective. In 1981, Mr. Williams was feeling deeply reflective; autobiographically so. That's when the third installment of the triptych of his autobiographical plays came to be with *Something Cloudy, Something Clear*. *The Glass Menagerie* exists in a space of the St. Louis years, followed by *Vieux Carré* in the first New Orleans period, before the protagonist goes west to be swept up into inevitable success. *Something Cloudy, Something Clear* completes the composite portrait that is Williams' origin story.

Something Cloudy takes place in Provincetown and centers on a writer named August. Here, Mr. Williams breaks with the convention he set of using TW as the initials for the protagonist, and opts for the name that suggests a soon-to-be-awakened greatness. Aside from the August narrator/protagonist, the names of characters drawn from Williams' life are unchanged—that's a noteworthy departure. Characters like Frank Merlo, Kip, and Tallulah Bankhead are unabashedly depicted. Williams addresses them as historical characters in the voice of August rather than layering on a veneer of fiction. Merlo appears in his final days, giving Williams a chance to say what perhaps he wishes he had. He hashes out with Tallulah Bankhead a fight they had years ago, which he was clearly still dwelling on. He sets to life onstage the boy he lost, Kip.

August is working on a play for the Theatre Guild in the action of *Something Cloudy, Something Clear,* drawn directly from Williams' time in P-Town. The line between reality and fiction becomes razor-fine with this drama that was staged for several months at the Jean Cocteau Repertory Theatre from 1981 to '82. *Something Cloudy, Something Clear* exists in the same category of fantasias as *Kirche, Küche, Kinder* and *Merriwether* because it stretches the bounds of reality and time onstage. *Something Cloudy, Something Clear* implements flashbacks and fast-forwards, which is unique among Tennessee Williams' plays, although they're commonplace in the work of hundreds of writers in the years to follow.

Another fantastical play in which Williams uses flashbacks and ghosts of real people is 1980's *Clothes for a Summer Hotel.* In *Clothes,* Williams chronicles the lives of novelist F. Scott Fitzgerald and his wife, Zelda Fitzgerald, with the central setting being the gates of the sanitarium Zelda died in. They recount high and low points in their marriage before eventually disintegrating into their immortal futures. In many ways, the play is similar to an earlier one-act called *Steps Must Be Gentle* in which the poet Hart Crane is visited by his mother, Grace, on the bottom of the ocean after her death. Hart had been dead for some years before Grace died, so this was their final confrontation—not dissimilar to the circumstance of the Fitzgeralds, since they had been apart prior to Scott's death, a couple of years before Zelda died. This handful of literary characters is unique, as Williams seldom wrote about historic figures, with D. H. Lawrence being a notable exception.

Like Scott and Zelda's ghosts as they make their entrances, *Clothes for a Summer Hotel* was dead upon arrival. It lasted just fifteen performances and was Tennessee Williams' last attempt at a Broadway opening. It would be all regional, finally, from here on out. Next chronologically was *Something Cloudy, Something Clear* downtown, and then a unique spin: Williams' adaptation of a play by Anton Chekhov with *The Notebook of Trigorin* in 1981. For more about this, turn to Appendix Y for Chekhov and the Desperate Unspoken further into this book. *Trigorin* played in Vancouver, and then Williams hopped down to Chicago to turn out one more Mississippi play.

A House Not Meant to Stand is a return to Williams' signature magical realism in Mississippi. It's the coast, not the Delta, but it's close enough. It includes lost, eccentric Southern characters at the ends of their ropes and a living situation that is literally becoming untenable. The house that is not meant to stand is falling apart around the McCorkle family that resides within. In *House,* Williams showcases his astonishing wit in satirizing a bevy of Southern tropes.

Cornelius, the man of the house, decides a night of a torrential deluge is the right time to start a row with his wife, Bella, whose mind is deteriorating fast. He understands that the house can't last forever, so he demands that Bella tell him where she keeps her nest egg. Her nest egg is moonshine money from her grandfather. She refuses to tell Cornelius where the money is hidden, whether because of her dementia or just because she's obstinate. Cornelius threatens her with institutionalization, which was the fate of their daughter (picking up on some of those old Tennessee Williams callbacks, are we?). At the height of their fraught stalemate, their youngest son, Charlie, always the ne'er-do-well, reappears from a long absence, forcing the couple to at least pretend as though things are normal around the house—ignoring the stress on them personally and the stress on the house from the elements outside.

Charlie has his own stressor to add to the mix: he's impregnated a Holy Roller—that is, a deeply religious young woman from another town. Hijinks ensue as the McCorkles gradually come around to various negotiated truces and agreements because, well, they have to. It's a rare happy-if-not-happy/ dismal ending in the Williams canon and a loving send-up to the state that bore him and impressed on him its weird and wonderful idiosyncrasies.

House was presented at the Goodman Theatre in downtown Chicago in 1982. That same year, Williams finally received some love from Boston, the town that might have slain him, when he is awarded an honorary degree from Harvard University.

Points of Interest

- In 1979, *Kirche, Küche, Kinder* is presented in a workshop by the Jean Cocteau Repertory Theatre.
- In 1980, *Clothes for a Summer Hotel* flops on Broadway and *Will Mr. Merriwether Return from Memphis?* enjoys a limited run at the Tennessee Williams Performing Arts Center in Florida.
- Edwina Dakin Williams dies in 1980 at the age of 95.
- In 1981, the highly autobiographical play *Something Cloudy, Something Clear* debuts at the Jean Cocteau Repertory Theatre and *The Notebook of Trigorin* is presented at the Playhouse Theatre in Vancouver.
- In 1982, the Goodman Theatre produces a limited run of *A House Not Meant to Stand.*

Tennessee Williams was found dead on February 25, 1983. He had been staying at the Hotel Elysee in New York City with a traveling companion who served as an assistant and secretary, John Uecker. He asked that he not be disturbed on the night of the twenty-fourth, no matter what disturbance might be heard. His wish was honored, and the next morning, Williams was gone, leaving only a body where his spirit once dwelt. Thousands crowded outside the hotel when the news broke to pay their respects.

Dakin Williams decided it was most fitting that Tennessee be buried next to their mother in St. Louis, a place that Tennessee Williams admittedly did not care for. Nothing seemed to work out right, since Tennessee in his life had stated that he wanted to die in the big bed he and Frankie shared in New Orleans and to be buried at sea like his favorite poet Hart Crane. There are reasons for fury, but the writer was gone.

The *New York Times* called him the "Poet of the Human Heart" in its remembrance of him. That was what was left. An impression on the human spirit where he had elevated it for a space of time. The handprint that Williams left on a generation of theatregoers, theatre-makers, and readers remains, long after his final keystroke on one of his myriad ramshackle typewriters.

What's almost as miraculous as the adventures he took us on is that his legacy wasn't buried with him by the circumstances that followed . . .

Scenic Route

It's purely conjecture, but had Williams been more interested in the regional theatre movement that began in the 1960s, he might have enjoyed a career more akin to famous playwrights today: that is, when a playwright of note has a show worth mounting, and Broadway isn't ready for it (or vice versa), a prominent regional theatre is often a solid place to build a foundation, workshop, and spread positive word of mouth. Some of Williams' shows did play out of town (and some never got *to* "town") in the last decades of his life, but the reluctance to market his work in those distant lands may have resulted in missed opportunities for longer runs and better receptions of strong plays dubbed poor by a hostile New York crowd. We will never know. Blame is certainly useless in this conjecture, since Williams also had representation to consider—first with Audrey Wood through 1970, then with Bill Barnes after Audrey, and a string of other agents who would never serve him as courageously and faithfully as the indomitable Audrey Wood. Gone, too, was his champion Margo Jones, who died back in the 1950s from having inhaled chemicals left in her home after having her carpet cleaned.

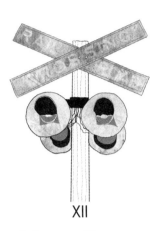

XII

NEXT STOPS

On February 27, 2015, I co-founded the Tennessee Williams Theatre Company of New Orleans with Nick Shackleford. The coincidence was not lost on me that February 27 is two days after the anniversary of Williams' death, but that was the day that we got an appointment with the Arts Council in New Orleans. We incorporated that day and set to work building a theatre production company dedicated to the works of Tennessee Williams—something that had been hedged around and hinted at for several years by other groups and individuals, but never executed with the focus of TWTC, as we have come to call it. Rather than paying homage to and doing works inspired by Tennessee Williams with a peppering of Williams' plays in the mix, we dove straight into Williams' oeuvre.

We didn't shy away from the lesser-known plays or the "weird stuff." We knew something that our audience would come to find out: Williams' body of work was plenty big enough to fill years of programming. We were cognizant of a landscape we were stepping into: one where Williams' breadth of imagination seemed only to have expanded after his death in 1983.

Thirty-two years and two days after Tennessee Williams' death, we entered a still-burgeoning cultural realm surrounding America's greatest playwright. Festivals, theatre artists, and scholars have used the three decades and beyond since Williams' departure to sculpt a fantastic, elaborate latticework of conversation about Williams' life and legacy. Those bravely keeping the light on for the dramatist include the Tennessee Williams/ New Orleans Literary Festival (founded in 1986); the Mississippi Delta Tennessee Williams Festival in Clarksdale, Mississippi (founded in 1993); the *Tennessee Williams Annual Review* (a publication begun in 1998); the Tennessee Williams Tribute in Columbus, Mississippi (founded in 2001); the Provincetown Tennessee Williams Theater Festival (founded in 2006); the New York Tennessee Williams Festival and Key West Tennessee Williams Festival (both of which lasted only a few years); and the St. Louis Tennessee Williams Festival (founded in 2016)—to say nothing of the multitude of biographies, fan fiction, and various compendiums and encyclopedias compiled by lovers and historians. These groups, authors, and publishers had already scouted ahead and observed that the market not only existed for theatre aimed at lovers of Williams, but they confirmed, too, that it was robust.

We were welcomed, in some cases with a little skepticism, by people and groups who shared our love for Tennessee Williams and theatre. The theatre folk were easy to win over—more opportunities to play on Williams' playground excites show folk. Some portions of the Williams crowd were apprehensive at first—they weren't sure there was enough love of Williams to go around, or there was question as to whether *all* of Williams' work was worthy of being staged. Quickly, we all learned that there was an abundance, much to everyone's benefit . . . and besides, no one owns a playwright.

Or do they? In the years immediately following Tennessee Williams' death, a sinister chill came over his legacy. The chill threatened the legacy itself, placing it in danger of fossilizing entirely. This unnatural ice age was cast by an enchantress with immense sway and an inordinate amount of free time to wreak havoc on our hero's history. There was a curse on Williams' story, following its end. Perhaps it's because the end, as many still believe it, is a lie.

Tennessee Williams choked on a bottle cap. That's what they said. He was found dead on the floor of his hotel room, an eyedropper cap or a pill bottle lid lodged in his throat—I've read it described both ways. He had a habit, the story goes, of opening pill bottles (eye drops?) with his teeth, and on that fateful night at the end of February 1983, he misjudged the force of his own prying, and the cap became lodged in his airway, suffocating him. It completed the narrative Williams had his whole life and throughout his work, regarding a fear of strangulation and suffocation. Breathlessness was a motif of his heroes, after all. Ever since that bout of diphtheria in his youth, Williams was phobic of not being able to breathe. How fitting, then, that his real-life demise would so closely resemble what his fictional characters dreaded so much? But there's just one hitch with this story.

Tennessee Williams *did not* choke on a bottle cap. That's what they said, but it's simply not true. Dr. Elliot Gross, New York's chief medical examiner at the time of Williams' death, fabricated the bottle cap story and later went back to the report to amend it. Williams died of Seconal poisoning, not asphyxia. Williams would join Judy Garland in being former patients of Dr. Max Jacobson to have died of Seconal overdose, having become addicted to the drug he favored prescribing.

But why would Gross wait six months to return to the document and change the cause of death, and to amend to something much more plausible? Perhaps it was because by that point, the newspapers had already run the story, reported asphyxia, and nobody would ever look back. That is, nobody except the forensically savvy Tennessee Williams nuts. Regardless of the wherefores, Gross was later shut down for making other false claims, so it seems to have been a habit of his.

A presumptive theory is that Williams' companion at the time couldn't bear the notion that the playwright's already tenuously positioned reputation could not take the damage of something resembling a suicide or drug overdose. It would confirm what all of the ugly stories since the 1960s had claimed: that Williams was a drugged-up drunk who pissed away his promise, destined to meet an addict's wasted end. So, why not lie and save his corpse the humiliation? Such clandestine and curious dissembling surely invites further intrigue, and maybe that lie spawned the curse.

Enter the Lady.

The Lady Maria St. Just was once an actor. Through force of will, she was able to insert herself into the actorly and writerly ponds that Tennessee Williams swam in. Like a "good actress" is taught to do, she ingratiated herself to Williams by drinking with him, dishing with him, camping with him, and seeming to hate all the people with whom he was quarreling at all the right times.

They became fast friends in the height of his fame, and while they were never *best* friends, she was a constant from that moment on. At one time, she capitalized on his insecurity and played on his fear of being washed up earlier in their friendship, but that appears to have ceased in the 1950s (she got wise, one suspects, that she'd lose her tether to relevance if she didn't play nice). Williams forgave her trespasses, and Maria became one of the angels in his corner, or so he thought. In Williams' strongest times, she was amusing company. In his weakest times, she was an enabling sycophant. But she was constant. She had hitched her wagon to his star, and clung on for dear life.

Her constancy won her a special place in his con-stellation of guardian angels. In a strange way, I'm sure she was looking out for him, in her own crooked, self-serving way. In her book *Five O'Clock Angel,* St. Just spins a compelling tale of their deep friendship amid dubiously crafted letters and narrative. Wheth-er she was devilish or dauntless, Williams had affec-tion for Maria, and so he left her a role in his will.

Maria was to be part of a two-person team executing Williams' wishes. She took her job very seriously, being that there was a sum of money—not a small one—associated with the work she did, and ample authority over the production and conversation about Williams' written and staged work attached to the job. The genius in Williams' designation of Maria as executrix was in a caveat: she must ensure that Rose was well provided for.

Remember Rose? Of course, you do, dear reader. She had a lobotomy back in the 1940s, and for all that horror, she survived for several decades. She was part of her brother's life until his passing, and he made her comfortable in upstate New York at a residential facility. It was now Maria's job to continue Rose's care at Stony Lodge. So long as this duty was executed, Maria had free rein over Williams' estate—okay, sort of. She didn't *actually* have free rein, but she acted like it. What she did have was a fanatical devotion to her cause, nearly unlimited resources won from her marriage to a lord, and infinite free time—in this world, that's equivalent to omnipotence. She took the reality of Tennessee Williams and held it hostage, hoping to force reality to warp to her whim.

What she chose to do with her authority was micromanage. The executor with whom she shared duty was busy with other famous clients, so Maria wrought her will with little resistance. Thus, she set out on her quest to construct her perfect image of Williams. If anything she viewed as unflattering to *her idea of* Williams' legacy was going on, she saw to its speedy demise. She restricted scholars' access to material written by Williams, lorded over big budget productions of his famous plays, and even went so far as to personally redact with an X-Acto knife passages of Williams' correspondence, which were held in archives. While we can sympathize for her staunch stewardship of Williams' legend, it isn't hard to determine that she was misguided in her efforts.

The result was the chill of which I wrote earlier. After hitting enough walls, scholars, publishers, and theatre-makers were worn down and acquiesced to Lady St. Just. The most tragic story of this kind is that of Lyle Leverich, whose biography *Tom: The Unknown Tennessee Williams* was halted from publication by St. Just and her flying monkeys. When it was finally released, Leverich did not survive to complete the second volume. The story stops with the opening of *The Glass Menagerie,* and it's a damn fine book. It did not, however, please Maria.

Fortunately for Leverich and the rest of us,

Maria herself expired in 1994—two years before Rose. After that, an influx of pent up conversation took place, but the decade between when Williams died and when the discussion opened up in a meaningful way was devastating to the discussion itself, naturally. The curse had been lifted, but there was makeup work to be done so that Williams' vital energy not be lost to the sorceress's machinations.

To be fair, Maria *did* allow a handful of plays, screenplays, and stories to be released. These were materials one must deduce she deemed worthy of production, and which she felt fit into the narrative about Williams that she wanted to live on. After her death, a flood of previously unpublished works and thrilling new productions cast off the stale pall that hung over Williams' reputation.

Four volumes of one-act plays have since been published thanks to New Directions, James Laughlin's publishing company with whom Williams stayed his whole career. Many of these volumes feature plays that stretch the reader's conception of what type of material Williams wrote. Half a dozen full-length plays have premiered since Maria's death, and Williams' candid musings come through in the volumes of his letters and notebooks that have become available for public consumption. Now, the estate is managed by the University of the South at Sewanee, Tennessee. The university recognizes Williams' work as a cultural moment rather than what Maria saw: an opportunity for personal gain and a duty to uphold a stringent standard. Williams chose the institution because the Reverend Dakin was an alumnus of it.

Now, Williams belongs to the people of the world, not one woman with an agenda, no matter how well-intentioned she may have been. There have since been some other individuals who have popped up and, in their eccentricity, attempted to co-opt Williams' narrative for their own, but they have been mostly discredited throughout the Williams-scholarly community—save for one who, as I write this, remains at large and whose invented quotes are widely circulated.

Great troves of drama have been unlocked for new generations of theatre artists, and what I believe to be most exciting about this new age of Williams is this: the playwright was ahead of his time; now we have arrived at the time he wrote for. In recent years, some of Williams' more unusual works have become more widely produced, and with much less negative reception. I say "less negative" recognizing that it's not unqualified praise. There are those out there who still hold Williams to the standard he set forth with *Menagerie, Cat,* and *Streetcar* (and there always will be), but folks interested in new, exciting theatre seem to really dig Williams' plays from off the beaten path.

Moreover, some of the plays that earned ire or neglect in Williams' lifetime have actually become popular in the decades following his death. *Vieux Carré,* a monumental flop in the 1970s, has become recognized as a canon play. *The Mutilated,* which premiered alongside *The Gnädiges Fräulein,* has managed to work its way from beneath *Fräulein*'s mangled shadow and is now recognized as a stand-alone one-act sufficient for a night of comedic theatre in its own right. Even wacky *Camino Real* has garnered some love in recent years, and has become a favorite of college programs willing to put forth experimental, imaginative theatre with large casts.

The man may be dead, but the plays are very much still alive. Their messages continue to resonate and the commentary on human relationships is perennially relevant. As the heavily censored films from the 1940s and '50s fade into memory, the older idea of a "black-and-white" Tennessee Williams goes with them. The sexually timid (you can call it nuanced if you want; I won't) *Streetcar* starring Vivien Leigh is not the standard anymore, having been replaced with dozens of more electric productions by directors and dramaturgs for a new century.

Still, the history should be known. As much as I laud the efforts of diverse young individuals pushing Williams' stories forward, the truth of his life remains as thrilling as the fiction. Why else would we be here, sharing this story again? Knowing the hundreds of Easter eggs that Williams deftly hid in his plays are based in reality is part of the fun of seeing or working on his material. They're also what helps us to tether his imagined circumstances to universal reality and a history we share with him. We are able to trace a map of a mythic South that Williams created from imagination, but which is so real you can taste, smell, and touch it.

He speaks to the Mississippi that I came up in. I can still follow Tennessee Williams' footsteps. As years went by and I was invited to attend all of the festivals in some capacity or another, I could see the places and plays of Tennessee Williams in living color. Rather than confining the writer's body of work to black, white, and grey tones in aged production photos and period portraits, I've seen the plays brought to life by people and groups from as far off as South Africa and as close to home as Clarksdale, Mississippi. When there was a play I didn't get a chance to see, I staged it myself with my theatre company. He speaks to me from onstage, to readers who clasp his poems and stories in their hands, curled up wherever they may be, private with his truths. For someone who understood all our hearts intimately, he was somehow simultaneously unlike any other.

Tennessee Williams put New Orleans on the map. Tennessee Williams opened the American South up to the world and let them hear its many songs. He wove Mississippi mouth magic around the globe. He showed us Brando, and held up a lens that let women and gay men know that men *could* be sexualized onstage. He stood by other giants like Arthur Miller, William Inge, and Thornton Wilder on the shoulders of the hidden women that held him aloft—an agent who cared for him, a mother who kept his every scribbling, a scrappy director who pressed for his work to be staged, and a reader who saw his potential. He experienced staggering loss but never lost the spirit, even when it was just a lonesome ember. He blazed trails. He made mistakes. He was the poet of the human spirit because he was so human and appealed to our collective spirit.

Tennessee Williams the man is dead, but the spirit of Tennessee Williams, that indefatigable fugitive holding a candle in the dark, warm corners where we huddle for safety and understanding is still present.

That's why we still talk about Tennessee Williams.

Points of Interest

- On February 26, 1983, Tennessee Williams dies of Seconal intolerance and was found in the Hotel Elysee in New York City. The cause of death was listed as asphyxia, but was amended to the truth some months later.
- After Williams' death, Maria St. Just serves as part of a two-person team of executors of his estate. She suppressed scholarly conversation, publications of unreleased work, and productions that displeased her, letting only some material be published or released.

- The 1980s see posthumous publications of *Clothes for a Summer Hotel, Stopped Rocking and other Screenplays,* and *The Red Devil Battery Sign.* St. Just also unearths a handful of plays from Williams' apprentice period, but they were not published until later.
- Since 1986, The Tennessee Williams/New Orleans Literary Festival offers fans from around the world a gathering place and tribute to celebrate the playwright and his significance to the city.
- In 1993, the Mississippi Delta Tennessee Williams Festival is established to continue Williams' legacy in the region he made famous and called home throughout his childhood.
- St. Just dies in 1994 and her responsibilities pass to the hands of the University of the South in Sewanee, Tennessee, who maintains control and care of it to this day.
- In 1996, Rose Isabel Williams dies.
- The late 1990s and early 2000s give way to productions and publications of *Spring Storm, The Notebook of Trigorin, Not About Nightingales, Stairs to the Roof, Fugitive Kind,* and *Candles to the Sun.* Williams' poems and letters are also collected, published, and released during this period.
- In 2001, the Tennessee Williams Tribute and Tour of Victorian Homes in Columbus, Mississippi, is established, further cementing Williams' literary legacy in the American South.
- From 2005 to 2015, dozens of one-act plays by Williams are released in various volumes by New Directions.
- In 2006, Williams' collected journals are released in *Notebooks* compiled by Margaret Bradham Thornton and published by Yale University Press. They offer insight into decades of Williams' life, movements, and musings. The same year, the Provincetown Tennessee Williams Theatre Festival is founded.
- In 2015, The Tennessee Williams Theatre Company of New Orleans is founded by Augustin J Correro and Nick Shackleford.
- In 2016, the St. Louis Tennessee Williams Festival is established.

- As of 2020, there remain some Tennessee Williams plays that are unearthed, unproduced, and unpublished.

THE SCENIC ROUTE

The last scenic vista overlooks a looming question that I'm often asked: "Why Tennessee Williams, why now?"

This is a question I actually get in the theatre realm, not so much in the seminar setting. What the person asking is usually trying to get at is, "What makes Williams relevant now, years later, when there are other stories by other storytellers to be told?" The short answer could easily be "I dunno; why Shakespeare?" But that's not going to inspire anybody to curiosity or creativity. Here's the longer, truer answer.

Tennessee Williams really got people. And places. And words.

Tennessee Williams shared New Orleans with the rest of the world in *A Streetcar Named Desire.* With *The Glass Menagerie,* he provided poetic but audience-centered narration alongside challenging, expressive design and an experimental episodic structure to the Broadway stage in a bolder way than anyone before him. And somehow it all worked! With his heroines Amanda Wingfield, Blanche and Stella Dubois, Maggie "the Cat" Pollitt, and countless others, he showcased the American South with grit, sensuality, and painstaking poignancy to the international conversation. The living rooms and bedrooms of these desperate figures became a battleground for the souls of these Southerners. He presented a counterpoint to the stereotypes of all Southerners as provincial, mouth-breathing yokels. These hard-won campaigns of his ennobled more than any romanticized Lost Cause of decades past.

Plus, he did all of this without glossing over the ugliness inherent in his world. He showed the shame while elevating the South's most beautiful traits.

Whether Southern or not, his characters were bursting with truth and pain, tamped down under a failing lid of repression, just like the people who came out in droves to see the characters fret and thrash. These were characters that may have been subplot second bananas or background players in the works of other dramatists, but they—like the people sitting in the dark room drinking them in—lived in a world of light and shadow that had seldom been represented with such honesty and mercy. They were his Fugitive Kind: footnote people pouring off the page to become footmen in a war for human understanding. If that sounds lofty, it was. In these and other plays, he heightened family drama to something universal and sublime.

Anchored by anxiety and fear of the unknown, the people and places Williams wrote about could be at the same time out-of-this-world and firmly rooted in it. The duality of escape and entrapment enthralled generations and continues to yank at the heartstrings of viewers today. His beloved Fugitives couldn't evade the pressures of the ambivalent universe, and so they clung together or groped for safe harbor. They were the strange, crazed, and queer creatures who were more human than human.

Naturally, this put him in a precarious position. Tennessee Williams wrote about civil rights and gay themes when other great American writers could only skirt the subject for fear of reprisal. Williams took the reprisal in stride and never stopped pushing the envelope. That frightened people. It frightened him. His plays were labelled dirty. They sold out anyway. He won Pulitzer Prizes for his particular, brilliant brand of violence. He also introduced Marlon Brando's sultry stares and supple biceps to the world in an unabashed eroticizing of the male form, which had seldom been done before.

His life and legacy isn't all rave reviews and gay romps, though. Tennessee Williams was charmed with no shortage of personal tragedies and addictions, none of which entirely defined him or prevented his success or placement among the pantheon of the world's great writers. Instead of becoming mired in his trials and tribulations, Williams carved himself out using his creativity, empathy, and that Southern stubbornness he instilled in his various heroines. He absorbed and processed each blow and through some alchemy of spirit turned horror into beauty. He traced the scars left on this planet and its people into a map for his creations to walk upon. For a playwright who is often tagged among the most depressing, his optimism about people was damn-near unmatched. I suppose that's what they meant when they called him the "Poet of the Human Heart" upon his death.

Tennessee Williams was a poet who became successful as a playwright because his plays were unapologetically poetic. Like all good poetry, his plays strike a chord with their readers and viewers more profoundly than they expect. Once that chord is struck in audiences, a hunger was identified in the American zeitgeist for material that went beyond the kitchen sink and plumbed the pipes and drains that were our collective emotional guts. He never stopped being concerned with helping people to understand one another more truly. As sure as this kind of understanding was needed in Williams' lifetime, I am equally as certain writing the words that we will continue to need it as you read them. *That*—understanding—is why Williams, why now.

Acknowledgments

My greatest thanks go to my three guiding angels on my Tennessee Williams journey: Brook Hanemann, who activated my love for the author; Thomas Keith, who introduced me to the circles of Tennessee Williams lovers and has been my regular sounding board; and my husband, Nick Shackleford, who had the wild idea to start a theatre company with me all about Tennessee Williams.

Others who were instrumental in my collection and organization of material for this book include: Karen Kohlhaas, David Kaplan, and my editor, Devinn Adams; to say nothing of the authors who came before me with their exhaustive study, and whom are numbered in my bibliography. I hope I've been able to distill their labors in a way that honors them and captures my readers.

Antoinette de Alteriis and Nina Kooij at Pelican Publishing, who saw my live presentation and identified the opportunity to make a book of it also deserve my gratitude.

Without Tracy and Paul at the Tennessee Williams/New Orleans Literary Festival, my publishers might never have had the opportunity to meet me, so they, too, were an integral part of this process.

Then there's my family—Dad and Judy and my Nanny and Papa; they made me who I am—whatever that is.

Finally, my love and admiration goes to the theatre artists who keep me returning to Williams' oeuvre with their dedication, craft, and generosity of spirit; without them, I'd never have arrived at this point. Carol Sutton's face in the role of Marguerite Gautier on a postcard from our production of *Camino Real* on my refrigerator is a constant encouragement, and I thank her for her generosity onstage. She exists in a constellation of my stars onstage and off that is comprised of Janet Shea, Lillian J. Small, LaKesha D. Glover, Gwendolyn Foxworth, Diane Baas, Kate Kuen, Elizabeth McCoy, Rachel Whitman-Groves, Michael Gillette, Joey Olsen, David Williams, Adler Hyatt, Linnea Gregg, Mary Pauley, Tracey Collins, Margeaux Fanning, Hebert Benjamin, Ken Thompson, Beau Bratcher, Patrick Gendusa, Rene Broussard, Madeline Taliancich, Zeb Hollins III, Kimberly Norlin, Frederick Meade, Emily Russell, Meredith Owens, Andrew King, Casie Duplechain, Sean Richmond, Lauren Turner, Robert Alan Mitchell, Kyle Daigrepont, Levi Hood, Julie Dietz, Lin Gathright, Chris Grim, Kim Paul, John Lavin, Joshua Bernard, Lee Kyle, James Howard Wright, Jerry Johnson, Megan Whittle, Matthew Raetz, Xavier Juarez, Leigh-Ann Sallis, Dustin Gibson, Mary Wildsmith, Brenda Caradine, Melissa Duncan, Cherry Golden, Beth Bartley, Brenda Currin, Laura Beth Berry, Shane Tubbs, Drew Stark, Vicki Hill, Julia Delois, Nat Twarog, Judy Lea Steele, Francisco Pazo, Peppy Biddy, David B. Carter, Josh Chenard, and dozens more, if even that few. I am lucky to have been inspired by them all.

And Mississippi, where for all its flaws, that Beanstalk Country is where Williams and I share family roots and owe thanks.

Appendix W
THE "WAS HE" SECTION

Questions and Answers

At the end of my Tennessee Williams 101 presentations, I generally take ten or fifteen minutes for questions. This appendix is dedicated to answering several of the questions that come up, but don't fit tidily into any branch of the narrative—mostly because they have to do with external factors more than they do with Tennessee Williams himself. I usually do my best to answer these in a complete way, but for many of them, the answer is simply "We may never know." The questions have been paraphrased from their various incarnations so as to get at the heart of the inquiries I am often met with.

Was Williams an activist writer for the LGBTQ+ community?

Short answer: No, but kind of, maybe?

Longer answer: To write gay topics in the mid-twentieth century was in and of itself activism. By today's standards, it was lazy activism, but that's like blaming a brontosaurus for carbon emissions. The landscape of the 1950s through the late 1960s was so hostile toward queer people that many of today's young activists can't imagine it—at least not in the United States.

Simply living as an out gay man in the public eye was a dangerous and revolutionary stance.

Williams was assaulted on the streets of Key West for his sexuality, and heckled and sneered at by strangers and public figures regularly. In spite of the hostility, he put characters onstage that let gay audience members, as one audience member of mine once put it, "see that it wasn't just me." From onstage, Williams' characters reached out and down the aisles and activated awareness in other gay people that they were not alone.

Williams' inclusion of LGBTQ+ characters in his Fugitive Kind was activism. But he didn't do it with the intention of activism, based on any historical documents we have to study. So that's why my short answer is "No."

Then, there were the activists who came for him. They wanted him to be doing more to forward the cause. In the late 1960s and through the 1980s, as Williams' work became more internally and personally focused, there were gay people who expected him to use his platform to further the cause. They felt he had a responsibility to his people to use his megaphone. He didn't, so they felt betrayed. Neither stance was entirely wrong . . . it was just a Williams-esque tragedy of incomprehension.

He didn't publish pamphlets or march in the streets. He didn't make a pronouncement of gay affirmation from the National Mall. He didn't throw bricks at the Stonewall Inn, and so in the annals of the queer revolution, he was not a participant. He did, perhaps, help to activate some of those activists. So that's something. Every story cannot be about everything, always. In his way, Williams wrote into being a beacon for wayward LGBTQ+ people. He wasn't able to do it all. Had he been around longer, perhaps he might have.

What was he on when he wrote [insert play here]?

This is really the only question I often get that pisses me off.

He was on imagination. Next question.

Just kidding (but only a little bit). Tennessee Williams did not need drugs or alcohol to be creative. A simple Google search of "writers who did drugs" will lay out for you more stars than are in the heavens. Most writers have used substances; some many, some often; some excessively, some fatally. We do know that Williams met his end because of a drug (prescription, not illicit).

It's true that Williams was dependent on his prescriptions and occasionally sought relief from his existential issues with LSD, cocaine, marijuana, and most frequently alcohol. However, I would argue that Williams did much of his writing in a state of hangover rather than an altered state of consciousness. We may never be sure, but Williams claimed to do his writing primarily in the early morning hours—this was also witnessed by people who shared quarters with him. This would indicate that much of his drug use occurred *after* he finished writing, maybe when he'd exhausted the muse or just wanted a good time. Furthermore, his strangest writings by the gentry's standards occurred at the beginning of his adult writing career and at the end—both timeframes when he was using *less* drugs than in the middle years, particularly his "Stoned Age" in the 1960s.

Take for example *Camino Real* (1940s / '50s), *The Strange Play* (c. 1938), and *Kirche, Küche, Kinder* (c. 1979). *Camino,* which is a surrealist fantasia in American themes, is one play I am often asked the question, "What was he on when he wrote *that?*" And I honestly don't think there was much going on in the drugs department at that time in his life. It began as a sketch in the 1940s entitled *Ten*

Blocks on the Camino Real, and ultimately grew into the full-length play that was panned by critics when it opened in 1953. But *The Strange Play,* while shorter, is every bit as strange as *Camino,* featuring weird hags in cramped rooms collecting garbage, as well as space wars and accelerated aging. Based on when it was written, Williams *may* have been enjoying some marijuana when he wrote it, and surely he had some drink here and there, but black coffee seemed to be his primary motivator for the piece of odd science fiction.

Comparing *Camino* to *Kirche, Küche, Kinder,* one will find the former to be exceedingly tame in style and substance. But by the time Williams got around to *Kirche,* he had somewhat recovered. If not recovered, he was at the least not at his apex of substance abuse, designated in the mid-to-late-'60s. Plus, again, he did much of his writing in the morning, with coffee and maybe something for his nerves. Both works activate something in the viewer. Their fantastical departures from strict reality makes audiences think he *must* have needed some kind of chemical elevation to come up with it.

Writers have imaginations. I, myself, have never taken drugs I wasn't meant to on a doctor's orders in my life to this point, but I have written some bonkers stuff. To decide that Williams needed drugs in order to create is reductive, and relies on the tired trope that Williams was a strung-out mess, an idea propagated by ultra-conservative and homophobic figures of decades past, who couldn't have turned out enough creativity to fill a fictional bottle cap.

So the answer is imagination. He was on his imagination when he wrote the play. And coffee. And maybe that night he did some drugs, but the weirdness of his plays was not dependent on a foreign substance. He was weird enough just as God made him.

Was Blanche just a gay man in drag? (. . . or something like that.)

No. A certain subset of gay men seem—and have for decades seemed—to feel the urge to place Blanche in a campy box, going so far as to make her into a drag queen. They justify the Blanche-as-D.Q. theory by claiming that Williams wrote himself into his main characters, and so he is Blanche, and since Williams was a man, Blanche is a man—in spite of all of the evidence in the text to the contrary.

It doesn't stop with Blanche, but the reasoning follows the same logic. While it may be amusing to imagine your local drag grande dame playing an epic Williams role, the way this tends to be best executed is by crafting one's own adaptation of the play built for drag queens, as Williams' plays were decidedly not that.

When asked, Williams refuted the idea, going so far as to point out the play in which a drag queen is most evident, *And Tell Sad Stories of the Deaths of Queens.* That play follows a night in the life of Candy, a store clerk by day and a woman every hour she's off the clock. She wears stylish women's clothing and lives her life as a woman. If anything, Candy might better be described as a trans woman, since the only time she does not present as a woman is when she is in her "professional" setting. The play was written before contemporary terminology existed, so we have Williams' words to go on. Thus, Candy is a drag queen.

Williams in his lifetime did not object to people who were transgender playing roles for which they were appropriately cast—one might remember Candy Darling as Violet in *Small Craft Warnings.*

Darling's portrayal was not as a drag queen, though; she was a woman playing a woman; the actor was transgender. And that was that.

In *Kingdom of Earth,* Lot Ravenstock comes down the stairs for his death in the final tableau dressed in his mother's finery. This is arguably a moment of drag, but it is integral to the moment in the play, not the overarching narrative. In *Not About Nightingales,* a character named only "Queen" may be an allusion to him having been a drag queen, or simply that he was gay, and the word "queen" is bandied about to refer to one gay man by another, and has been for over a century. So, there may be evidence that drag queens other than Candy exist in Williams' work, but none of them occupy the space of significance that Candy does in her own story. Either way, if Williams had wanted to write a drag character, he would have done so, which he did. He personally gave evidence for when he had, and that's that; case closed.

*The only addendum I will make to this, from a theatrical production standpoint, is that if a play features a motley ensemble, such as *The Mutilated* or *Camino Real,* a drag queen might figure into the chorus . . . but to impose drag onto a non-drag scenario changes the overall symbolism, which you can read more about in Appendix Z.

Was he working out his personal problems when he wrote?

Oh, my, yes.

Was Williams bipolar? Depressed? Schizophrenic? Etc.?

I don't rightly know. I'm not a psychologist. He saw some, but they were summarily dismissed as quacks once the dust of history settled on their practices. Dr. Kubie told him to stop being gay and stop writing. He did neither. Rose's course of treatment included cutting into her brain. Psychology and psychiatry had some kooky ideas back in the day, and as much as we think we might be able to glean a diagnosis from his letters or his creative work, we can't and shouldn't.

Diagnoses should not be gleaned. Any doctor would tell you that. Especially when it comes to mental disorders, it's bad practice to posthumously diagnose a patient without any sort of interview or examination. Since we have neither, I say . . . let's just say he was admittedly troubled and anxious and be satisfied with that. I think it's more respectful.

Was [name of character] actually [name of person I heard of once], because I heard . . .

I'm going to stop you there and say, "We may never know." And that's not snark, it's just that we can't know for sure, unless Williams wrote about it, or someone documented it. As explained back in Part I, Williams crafted carefully constructed composites out of the fragments of reality that he knew, and melded them with imaginary features and circumstances. Some of his characters were more real than invented; others, the opposite.

Many people have met Williams or people who knew him intimately, and they all have stories and theories as to which parts of whom—from reality—made their ways into his work. Who wouldn't want some sliver of their story to be immortalized in a Tennessee Williams play, or poem, or story? But I try to keep a skeptical eye and ear on these things, and I encourage others to do the same. Action, dialogue, and other clues in the text are paramount. Anything biographical, while it may enrich one's understanding of the text, if it is not inherently in the text, is lagniappe. As fun as it is to imagine connections—*and it can be fun!*—it is just that: imagination.

I do, however, like to imagine that Williams infused the stardust of many people whose lives he touched into his plays. I believe that is what made them spellbinding and transformative. So while I try not to strictly confirm or deny Ms. Melba Winemiller, a spinster from the far end of Clarksdale who used to keep a trained monkey, and maybe inspired Alma from *Summer and Smoke* or inspired the father with the monkey from *Orpheus Descending* from having a stake in the plays (and primarily because I just made her up), I try more to navigate folks to look at the direct links. Like Blanche Cutrere and Williams' paternal aunt being shades with which he painted Blanche DuBois, or Sidney Lanier and Reverend Dakin sharing qualities with Reverend Shannon and Nonno in *Night of the Iguana*. Those are connections that check many of the boxes for a Williams composite—even if neither of them was known to have run off to marry a Stanley or be jilted by a Mitch.

This raises the other point I have, which I cannot stress enough, and gets answered in the next question.

Why are you so interested in Tennessee Williams?

I'll be honest, I used to hate Tennessee Williams.

Well, I hated the idea of him.

I mean, I hated the idea that I was expected to like him.

When I was a teenager in the Mississippi Delta, the strong expectation was that Tennessee Williams would be something I went in for, because of his cultural importance to the region. Naturally, being a rebellious teenager who knew better than everyone else, I bucked that expectation. When I was faced with Williams in classroom settings, first in high school, then in college, I met him with scorn.

Then came the production of *Summer and Smoke* that I was in. My first summer in Columbus—another Tennessee Williams-crazy place—I auditioned for a Williams play. Why? Because I was a young acting student, and I was taught to audition for everything, and take whatever role was given. The audition was for the play by Williams to be presented at the Tennessee Williams Tribute and Tour of Victorian Homes, and it was to be presented on one of the stages at my college. So, like an industrious theatre student, I auditioned and was subsequently cast. I played Roger Doremus, a dopey young man who didn't stand a chance of winning Miss Alma's affection. Looking back, I recognize that I was perfectly cast, even if the Alma and John were much older than they should have been, and the girl playing Rosa Gonzales was white (yikes).

Now you'd think I must love Tennessee Williams by now, getting to be in such a great play, and experiencing it for myself.

Nope. I hated it. I thought it was stiff, hokey, full of stereotypes, and for all the talk of heat, it felt cold. The production was sexless, as I look back on it now. There was no fire—no passion. There was a lack of chemistry all around, which is no less than might be expected from a community theatre production of an epic Williams romance. So, I went back to the classroom after that production still mad at Williams—doubly so! Now I had evidence, I thought, to justify my disdain for America's *least* great playwright—no, strike that! Its *most* greatly *overrated* playwright. So there!

The following semester, I had to study *The Glass Menagerie,* which was a chore since I was viewing it through the lens of that sad production of *Summer and Smoke.* Finally, my senior year at Mississippi University for Women, something changed. A young adjunct professor named Brook Hanemann joined the staff, and she was disappointed but challenged by my distaste for Mr. Williams. Long story shorter, it was a struggle, but about two weeks into her Women in Tennessee Williams seminar in the spring of that year, she had me examining Williams in a more curious light. Then the curiosity became admiration. She fixed my bad attitude.

I started to see that Williams had all the same issues with his South that I'd had with mine. The expectation, the hypocrisy, the bigotry, the stifling religion . . . it was all there. So, too, were the eccentricities and wonders. A fabulous new world opened up to me, and it only took me the better part of a decade to come around. After Brook's intervention, I consumed as much Williams as possible, then as much about Williams as I could. I went to my first Williams Festival in New Orleans the year following Hurricane Katrina and saw that I wasn't the only person who loved him for the reasons I've described.

I think lots of people had an easier time latching onto Williams because they didn't have my youthful pride to overcome about it. They saw themselves in the work immediately. They saw themselves reflected in the struggles of the people he wrote about and the situations he put them in. That is why he was the "Poet of the Human Heart," as he was described—he strikes those familiar cords we all share. He made a community out of fugitivity, forging an empire of understanding from isolation.

What are some of the themes that appear across many of his plays? Can you give some examples?

Like I said, I move quickly, and spend all of about three minutes discussing Williams' themes and topics before wrapping up. This question actually came to me in several incarnations, and so I boiled it down to a form I could answer using a list (more **Points of Interest!**). I like to think of topics being the noun, and themes being the sentences about the noun. Below, I'm listing the topics and breaking them down into themes, with explanations. Each of these occupy several plays by Williams.

- Desire
  - We are consumed by that which we desire.
  - Desire is the only thing that motivates us when we have nothing left.
  - Desire overpowers reason.
  - Desire is costly.

In *Streetcar,* we clearly see characters driven by a desire for something dangerous and potentially deadly. Blanche desired too much for a woman living in bucolic Laurel, so she was driven out. She comes to New Orleans and is conflicted between her desire (for danger, men, and drink) and her better judgment (a life with Mitch). Sadly, her past and present desires conspire against her to make a future impossible. Desire is personified in Stanley when he takes everything from her. Meanwhile, Stella's desire for Stanley blinds her to his sins and makes her forsake dignity and her sister. A similar desire stalks Tom Wingfield in *Menagerie,* as his drive to depart for adventures gnaws at him. He is placed at odds with his mother, who detects his plan, and eventually he has to face his guilt because he gave into his desire in spite of his responsibility. His guilt and remorse are reflected in his plaintive, retrospective monologues at the beginning, middle, and end of the piece.

In *Orpheus Descending,* Val and Lady's desire for something forbidden, perched precariously under the nose of her husband, results in both of their demises. Compounding the desire motif, the lovers' fate is arguably all because the women of the town so desired Val that they cast a sexual spotlight on him. It's a town that is set ablaze by desire, and the blaze leaves devastation.

In *Suddenly Last Summer,* the monologues describe a Sebastian Venable that was driven singularly by desires, and when his mother—the governess that protected him—is dispensed with, desire (and children) devour Sebastian. His desire is so destructive that its aftermath tears other people's lives apart.

As a counterpoint, in *Summer and Smoke,* Alma spends much of the play combatting her desire, thinking that she's winning. John Buchanan eventually sobers up and measures his desire. But by the time he's ready to come down to Alma's level, she has succumbed to the pressures of desire and has flown off like a phoenix, reborn through desire into something John can't hold.

Several characters equate desire with survival, and other characters capitalize on them. Hustlers, sex workers, and characters engaging in survival sex appear in *Sweet Bird of Youth, The Roman Spring of Mrs. Stone, The Milk Train Doesn't Stop Here Anymore, The Mutilated, Suddenly Last Summer* . . . you get the point. Sometimes the characters are more predatory than others, but the capitalizers all get something by exploiting those enthralled by desire. The transactional element supports the "desire comes at a cost" theme, especially when the cost is not just monetary, but spiritual or psychic.

- Fragility
  - Some people are too fragile for the world.
  - Fragile people often present strong or violent fronts.
  - The merciless world wears down strong people into fragile ones.

In *Streetcar,* Blanche, was burned up from her desire and worn down from being strong for her dying family for so long. She was reduced to something too soft to survive in the New Orleans environment. Stanley's crudity and straightforwardness burst her soap-bubble affectations, which were her last defense mechanism. She spends much of the play in a warm bath to soothe her nerves—reconstituting herself. Like the paper lamp that Stanley ultimately crushes, she is too fragile to be exposed even to direct light.

In *Menagerie,* Laura seems as breakable as her glass animals, and when one special piece is finally broken, it keeps time with her own hopes shattering. Everything in the Wingfield home is shown to have been extremely tenuous, since Jim's simple, candid words are able to smash so much of what Amanda had built and struggled to hold together.

In *Camino Real,* Kilroy (a representative of the American Dream) has a heart so large and unstable that any shock might kill him outright. He has to put on a masculine boxer's front all while being the most fragile creature on the desperate path. Several times during the play, the more poetic characters describe violets breaking the rocks—meaning that something rare and soft must be responsible for shattering the hardness of the world. That's ultimately what happens when Kilroy dies and is reborn as a great hope for the world. Kilroy is revived and Quixote awakens from his dream in concert with the flowers breaking apart far-off mountains.

In *Vieux Carré*, each character in Mrs. Wire's rooming house is in a more precarious position than those beneath them. Her collection of exotic people struggle with sickness, poverty, starvation, and longing. She has amassed her own menagerie of breakable people, and struggles to keep them inside lest the outside world destroy them like it did her long-lost son.

- Inheritance/Legacy
  - All that is left after the fighting's done is our legacy.
  - Legacy is sometimes all that we can leave others to inherit when there's nothing of us left.
  - When we die, we leave behind more than just money and material things.

In *Cat on a Hot Tin Roof,* the characters are all struggling to stay on top of the pile when it comes to Big Daddy's legacy—an inheritance to take care of them. Every character needs the money, but Brick is not concerned because of his addiction and guilt. It falls to Maggie to champion Brick, and she struggles against those with more of a claim than she has, each of whom is poised to dead-leg her or Brick to get the inheritance. It's a game of King of the Hill, but their hill is a gurgling volcano.

In *Suddenly Last Summer,* Sebastian's inheritance is what's being sought by the Holly family, and being held over their heads by Violet Venable. She uses the inheritance and their hunger for it as a weapon against Catharine, just like Sebastian holds money over young men to get what he wants. Violet is more concerned with protecting Sebastian's poetic reputation than what happens with the capital. Her privilege is her greatest leverage.

In *Summer and Smoke,* it takes the death of

his father for John Buchanan to realize that his legacy matters. He turns his life around, settles down, and becomes the "Good Doctor" his father had been, and which the community needed. His father's legacy becomes the role he must fill, as he is assimilated into the homogenous world.

- Reputation
  — Protecting a reputation can come at a heavy cost.
  — Reputation is our lasting legacy.
  — Reputation must be upheld.

Suddenly Last Summer pits reputation of the dead against the safety of the living when Violet becomes so fixated on the implications of Catharine's account of Sebastian's death that she will stop at nothing to silence the girl.

In *The Rose Tattoo,* Serafina is so concerned with her reputation and the reputation of her dead husband that she goes into a years-long period of grief to prove her devotion to Rosario. It is at the expense of her daughter's social life that Serafina proves her undying devotion. She even goes so far as to bury the lede (she thinks) that her husband was cheating on her in order to uphold the idea that they were a perfect match.

Blanche is so terrified that her reputation will follow her from Laurel in *Streetcar* that she painstakingly fabricates alibis and half-truths, which she has at the ready when she's met with questions. She cannot stand the thought that her illusions of propriety will be savaged, and so she hangs onto them even as she is carted off to the booby hatch, triumphantly putting on one more act for the poker players in her famous exit line.

In *The Milk Train Doesn't Stop Here Anymore* and *Sweet Bird of Youth,* older actresses are consumed by their imagined reputations to the point of isolation. Similarly in *Summer and Smoke,* Alma isolates herself in order to maintain her reputation as a "good girl" in spite of her growing desire.

- Escape
  — The world is a place to escape from.
  — There is no escape from captivity.
  — The self is the one inescapable thing.
  — Escape is impossible when pursued.

Almost every one of Williams' full-length plays features some drive for escape: In *Camino Real,* all characters hope to escape the titular road; in *Streetcar,* Blanche has arrived in New Orleans to escape her past; in *Night of the Iguana,* Shannon has come to the end of the world to evade the demons that seem to follow him. Captivity becomes a theme each time a cage appears: the prison in *Not About Nightingales,* the display shelf filled with animals in *The Glass Menagerie*, the metaphorical roof in *Cat on a Hot Tin Roof.* Entrapment is also commonly explored—*In the Bar of a Tokyo Hotel, Period of Adjustment, Kingdom of Earth,* and so on.

Williams knew that the spirit of mankind often feels trapped, or that it needs to move. His plays shone a lamp on this topic and highlighted these themes, creating a beacon for those other wave-tossed fugitive travelers to know they weren't alone in the long tempest.

It's worth bringing into this examination of escape, Williams wrote bird imagery into several of his plays, and typically they symbolized some kind of escape, fly, or flee. Birds come second to roses in the compendium of Williams imagery. Crack a Williams play, and you're likely to find roses or birds used—happy hunting!

Appendix X

WHAT HAPPENS IN THESE PLAYS?

Sometimes in the course of this text, in order not to interrupt the flow of the narrative of Williams' life, I have omitted descriptions of some significant plays. Usually, this was because the events surrounding the plays were more relevant than the material in the plays to the greater arc of Williams' story. That doesn't mean they're not important. Below are the descriptions assigned to some of the plays mentioned that you couldn't say you read *Tennessee Williams 101* without encountering.

The Milk Train Doesn't Stop Here Anymore (1963)

Flora Goforth is a fading diva suffering from a chronic disease that is never fully explained. She has come to a villa on a cliffside on the southern coast of Italy to thrash out her last days and complete her memoirs. At heart, she professes to be a "Georgia swamp bitch" and wears her status as a dragon lady with great pride. She's abusive to her secretary, a woman named Blackie (Frances Black; semantically it would be easy to mistake a servant called Blackie as a stereotype of a maid. This is not the case, but the name makes one look twice), and the handful of employees who scurry around the villa at her service. One day, Flora's surprised to find that a foolish vagrant has been attacked by her guard dogs coming up the side of the cliff to pay her a visit.

Flora, or Sissy as she claims her friends call her, is understandably surprised when a stranger has come to call on her. She sends Blackie to spy on the youth named Chris Flanders. He's a young-but-not-too-young sculptor (Williams' men always have some kind of artistic trade) who alleges he met Sissy at some point in the past. We soon come to find out that other women Chris has visited have come to refer to him as the "Angel of Death." When Chris visits old ladies, they die not long after, and Chris is financially provided for, having swept in during the women's dying moments to comfort them. He sees it as a vocation and a curse. Sissy sees it as a hustle.

Gradually, Sissy grows fond of Chris and realizes that her death is inevitable; that his company cannot harm her. She tells him parts of her story too painful and too well-guarded for her memoir, and slides off the mortal coil in his comforting presence.

Stylistically, Williams was experimenting with Japonica at the time, implementing use of Kabuki-style stage assistants to usher off props and announce parts of the action and meaning of the play from time to time. It's an imperfect use of Eastern elements, which became a minor trend for Williams during the 1960s and '70s. For more regarding this topic, hop back to Part IX and read about *In the Bar of a Tokyo Hotel.*

This Is (An Entertainment)

This Is (An Entertainment) for Maria St. Just was the full, original title of the play. Maybe she would have appreciated that the play was vaudevillian in its style, crude in its wordplay and situations, and heavy-handed in its metaphors. Or maybe it was a loving jab. We will never know. Perhaps she didn't put two and two together to figure out that the Countess, the antiheroic protagonist of the play, was a social climbing ogress not unlike herself. Or maybe I'm reading that into it. Either way, when the play opened in California in 1976 for a brief run, it was billed just as *This Is (An Entertainment).*

The play reads much like *Cairo! Shanghai! Bombay!,* Williams' first produced play. In *Cairo!,* a pair of sailors are out on shore leave looking for some loose women. It's a cruder, more rudimentary take on the situation from Betty Comden and Adolph Green's musical *On the Town,* and it features several vaudeville tropes. *This Is* features a loose-legged Countess looking for action in a nondescript European tourist town on the eve of a great conflict in some unnamed war. She enlists her driver's help, and finds out he has a twin brother who is leading a revolution against the powers that be—powers she relies on for her social standing.

This Is, filled with vulgar humor and ground-level jokes, played against the opulence of the setting and the Countess's airs. She succeeds in finding sex, but the conflict of the state is not avoided. It's a fun read, and if you lay hands on it, I recommend reading it aloud—it comes off less dense that way.

Tiger Tail

This stage mutation of *Baby Doll* is much the same in substance as the screenplay for the film, but features considerably more local flavor. The people from the Delta community have more of a presence, and there are some secondary characters introduced who give the world a fuller, more complete feeling than the intentionally contained action of the movie. *Tiger Tail* has all the trappings of *Baby Doll:* Archie, Silva, and, of course, Baby Doll herself, but there's special emphasis put on the social setting, creating a more broad commentary on the mythic South Williams is known for having crafted.

Red Devil Battery Sign

Red Devil is part-thriller, part-fantasy. Opening like a Texan version of *In the Bar of a Tokyo Hotel,* the Woman Downtown is presented as a dark, mysterious, and deeply anxious Williams heroine. She was physically and psychically tortured by her power-hungry industrial magnate husband, whose Red Devil Battery company obliquely represents an oppressive, conservative industrial American culture.

In the bar, she meets a virile, talented mariachi singer named King Del Rey, but as they get to know one another through the course of the play, she learns that his blush of life conceals a history of illness. He has recovered from brain cancer, but expects his days are numbered. The Woman Downtown is drawn to King because she sees him as a way out of her bondage to her Red Devil—plus there's kinship, as she had her brain injured in another way: electroshock therapy.

As King and the Woman talk, there is an ever-intruding red light from across the street beaming into her hotel room, which is the neon sign of the Red Devil Battery Company. In the cold, red glow like a shadow of imminent discovery, they abandon caution and hatch a plan for the Woman to escape, and for the King to join his daughter, a singer, on the coattails of her bright future.

In true Williams style, it all comes crashing down when the Woman's plan is foiled not by her power-mad husband, but by the King's sudden death and her kidnapping from wild forces outside of the hotel. She is taken off into an uncertain world to be the prize of a gangster—safe from the Red Devil

Battery Sign, but terrified of what new terrors the future holds.

Red Devil echoes a rebuke of the military-industrial complex that Williams made a few times, dating all the way back to *Me, Vashya,* a short play of his from the 1930s. Surely feeling the cyclical return to a predatory system that sacrificed the individual for war and profit, Williams returned to this topic that he had explored in the pre-War period once again following the devastating Vietnam War. In what was his most overtly political move, possibly ever, Williams spoke at a rally organized by fellow writer Norman Mailer in 1971 against the war.

A THEATRE-MAKER'S PRIMER ON STYLE AND INFLUENCE —OR— *FURTHER,* FURTHER READING

Dear Reader,

There are two reasons for you to read beyond this point: If you, as a curious being, are interested in a more in-depth understanding of Williams' work as a theatre-maker, specifically, or if you are a theatre-maker. Or you could be both (Huzzah!). But for those of you who may not have any distinct yearning to plunge into the murky waters of the stage artiste, the following two appendices may read a little dense and wonky. That's fine, too. I provide this for those persons who may want a tad more of a "Theatre of Tennessee Williams 101" experience.

Yours always,
The Tennessee Williams Nerd

An Insightful Performance and the Ibsenesque Catastrophe

Williams saw a production of Norwegian playwright Henrik Ibsen's *Ghosts* when he was a university student, and he explained how this production was a revelation to him in journals. The play expresses themes on the notions of sins of the father and pasts that come back to haunt characters, not dissimilar themes to Williams' own favorites.

The widow, Helen Alving, was repeatedly cheated on by her husband. After his death, Helen hopes to spend up all of her dead spouse's money on an orphanage. In doing so, she will prevent her son, Oswald, from inheriting a cent from her philandering husband, freeing him of any link from the cursed rake. She later learns that her son is suffering from syphilis, which she believes to have been inherited from his father (that's not how syphilis works, but okay). Matters are made worse when the Widow Alving is introduced to Oswald's girlfriend, whom the widow knows to be his half-sister, another curse her husband left behind to haunt the family. The girl, Regina, breaks off the relationship and Oswald is devastated. His health declines, and he begs his mother to kill him with morphine if he begins to suffer too much and lose his mind (syphilis was yet incurable). The Widow Alving is left to face a horrible choice at the conclusion of the play.

Throughout *Ghosts*, Ibsen filled Helen Alving with complexity and conflict, which titillated Williams—compounded by the performance of Alla Nazimova, whom he saw in the role. Long-past mistakes and sins encroaching on the future, husbands whose legacies cause suffering beyond their departures, and women of substance and desperation would become staples in Williams' own plays, especially in his apprentice years after he saw *Ghosts*.

Ibsen focused on family conflict, class castes, and themes of past sins being inescapable and fulfillment of social expectation at any cost. The price was often a catastrophic collapse in the dynamic toward the end of the plays that left characters and audiences reeling. Two other plays highlight this theme: *Hedda Gabler* and his most famous work, *A Doll's House*. Both bear striking resemblances to the domestic situations and topics explored in Williams' work.

The titular protagonist in *Hedda Gabler* is trapped in a situation that will humiliate her husband, the writer George Tesman. Recently married and on the precipice of marital and professional bliss, the Tesmans' situation becomes suddenly desperate. The trouble begins when a rival of George's, Eilert Løvborg, resurfaces after a decade-long bender. It is revealed Eilert is a past lover of Hedda's, of which George is unaware. To sabotage her ex and ensure George isn't threatened, she secretly burns Eilert's precious manuscript. Eilert is devastated, and Hedda capitalizes on his misery by recommending he kill himself. When he does, Hedda is riddled with guilt and finds herself feeling more desperate than before. Worse, a mutual friend recognizes the pistol as George and Hedda's, and threatens Hedda with exposure—and the house with scandal, the most mortal of sins. From what seemed like the verge of a perfect life, Hedda is flung into an anxious and untenable pit. She resolves the circumstance by killing herself, leaving her friends so shocked that the only statement one can muster is "People don't do such things." This grotesque commentary on social expectation relates to many of Williams' play endings, e.g., the mobs lynching Chance Wayne and Val Xavier in *Sweet Bird* and *Orpheus/Battle,* respectively. Hedda driving Eilert to suicide is also similar to Blanche and Alan's last exchange in *Streetcar.*

In *A Doll's House,* Ibsen's characters are again cast as social something-or-others, tasked with living up to the expectations of the society in which they circulate. Nora and Torvald Helmer are a happily married couple on the surface: nice home, sweet children, loving relationship, and other trappings of domestic bliss. What Torvald doesn't know is that Nora has a past that she's done a great job at concealing—one that (you guessed it) resurfaces in the action of the play and jeopardizes the perch on which they sit. Once upon a time, Nora took out a loan (—*Quelle horreur!*—a *woman* making a fiscal transaction) and now the term is suddenly up. Her lender has been fired by Torvald himself, and so blackmail is afoot. After some suspenseful scenes, everything is resolved moneywise, but something curious and groundbreaking happens. Through her trials and tribulations, Nora learns that Torvald is a weak, unworthy man. She tells him so, announces her discontent, and leaves Torvald and their children. The exit of Nora from the Helmer home was termed "The Door Slam Heard 'Round the World" because of its groundbreaking portrayal of a woman defying expectation and doffing her social station. The ending of *The Glass Menagerie* smacks of this type of departure, when Tom Wingfield, having spent the whole play remaining in the household out of duty, decides to vacate without keeping his promise to ensure his sister's security.

Similar to the seemingly flip or inappropriate curtain line in *Hedda Gabler,* Blanche triumphantly declares at the end of *Streetcar,* "Whoever you are, I have always depended on the kindness of strangers." This line has often escaped the understanding with which Williams appears to authored it. He saw it as a punch line of sorts. Blanche breaks with reality one final time to give a final middle finger to the gauche and ambivalent universe of the Kowalski home. She decides not to acknowledge defeat, but rather to accept the doctor's help on her own terms, off to her next grand adventure—and completely in control. She's not being ironic or sarcastic, and she doesn't outwardly appear to be fraught any longer. Williams more than once had exit lines that did justice to the character or the commentary rather than the situation. Like Ibsen's final line in *Hedda Gabler,* he struck at a closer truth by not being maudlin and distraught over horrible circumstances, and instead chose to make statements about the spirit of the people surviving.

Menagerie perfectly illustrates a type of dramatic moment, which I've dubbed the "Ibsenesque Catastrophe." This convention is when the buildup in the rising action moves toward resolution, then everything comes crashing down just after the climax. Devastation is substituted for resolution. In *Menagerie,* it's the moment in which Laura learns that Jim is engaged to be married to a girl named Betty, whom we never meet. The glass unicorn breaks, the metaphorical sky falls, and Amanda and Laura are left devastated at the exact moment things should have taken an upswing for the Wingfields. Audiences who don't know *Menagerie* already—students I've taught in high school, for example—are just as shocked by the introduction of the phantom Betty as audiences were when Nora left Torvald holding the proverbial bag. I'll never forget fifteen-year-old Danae blinking and blurting "The fuck is *BETTY?!*" and being mad about it for three solid days.

Menagerie wasn't an answer to *A Doll's House* or *Hedda Gabler* per se, but the emotionally explosive Ibsenesque Catastrophe paired with the standard bearers of societal expectation certainly suggest marks of Ibsen's influence. Even if there's not much direct correlation, the overarching impact Ibsen made on mid-century dramatic standards was in play. Ibsen is regarded as one of the first significant dramatists of the Modern era and the Father of Realism, too. Williams was reared in the Modern Realist conventions and the departures he made into Magical Realism and Expressionism would not have been possible without the foundation that Ibsen, O'Neill, and other writers of note had laid out.

Other examples of Ibsenesque Catastrophe include:

- Lady and Val being snatched from the jaws of a happy ending and instead being murdered and lynched in *Orpheus Descending.*
- Maggie roping Brick into a pregnancy ruse in order to lock down a stability that is dissatisfying to him in *Cat on a Hot Tin Roof.*
- Chance Wayne getting ditched by his patron and then snatched up before he can escape town in *Sweet Bird of Youth.*
- Alma being ready to be with John Buchanan after all those years only to find that he's settled for Nellie at the end of *Summer and Smoke.*

Anton Chekhov and the Desperate Unspoken

Williams admitted that his greatest influence as a dramatist was Anton Chekhov, the Russian playwright who famously authored *The Seagull, Uncle Vanya, Three Sisters,* and *The Cherry Orchard.* Chekhov, like Williams, wrote social messages in the personal mode. Compared to Williams' contemporary Arthur Miller, who might write a play about a witch hunt as an overt metaphor for the trials being held by Joe McCarthy (*The Crucible*), Williams and Chekhov buried social messages in the circumstances of their plays. Williams' social messaging always played second fiddle to his broader themes about human relationships. Chekhov did the same, and with good reason. To have written more overtly might have gotten him thrown in the slammer, Russian society being what it was at the time.

In Chekhov's writings, young Tom Williams saw domestic situations that were microcosms for a changing economy and society. This type of narrative resonated for Williams, and much of his most successful work is an outgrowth of realism that had trickled into the American zeitgeist in the early to mid-twentieth century. Chekhov's plays were also championed by Russia as a nation, and were fodder for the most prominent acting teachers of the day—specifically Konstantin Stanislavski. Stanislavski's acting methods were disseminated and lauded as the best practices for actors for the greater part of a century, so naturally they informed Williams' understanding of what an actor's performance should look and sound like.

Situationally, *The Cherry Orchard* reads like a Russian prelude to *A Streetcar Named Desire.* The orchard represents for its occupants a way of life that is shifting into the provincial background in favor of cosmopolitan climes. Like Belle Reve in *Streetcar,* it is turning into a vestigial property, and not all of its inhabitants are prepared to become irrelevant. The standard bearers clash with inevitable fate while other members of the family and their workers prepare for a future that is quickly becoming their present. This is similar to Stella's decision to flee the mansion for New Orleans, only returning to her ancestral home to attend funerals while Blanche fights tooth and nail against the enemy, Time.

The Seagull, which Williams probably first encountered in the library in Memphis the summer of his 1933 breakdown, made an impact on him—enough so that he eventually adapted it in *The Notebook of Trigorin.* What we may infer was fascinating to Williams is its rich use of subtext to convey the depth of the relationships—and the suffering that comes from repressing big feelings— burying them, leaving them largely unexpressed.

It demands that actors play against what they say, or rather, what they're expected to say in various situations. This reveals their duplicity. Williams and Chekhov share something in common that can confound actors and directors: characters who lie and dissemble without explicit resolution. They forego dramatic irony, wherein the audience knows something the characters don't, and instead rely on behaviors and allusions to create suspense. Chekhov and Williams often rely on their audiences' emotional intelligence, which has a nice payoff, if the actors deftly illuminate the material. For example, to listen to Blanche tell it, she's a perfectly-behaved *young* woman. We have to rely on what's learned from other characters to discover her true behaviors—and even then, who can say for sure?

Characters in *The Seagull* ascribe to a similar method of communicating: a desperate, longing refusal to say what they mean except to just the right person. Keeping secret their feelings compounds their suffering. *The Seagull* parallels Williams' own experimentalism with form, too. The character Konstantin, who is a playwright, is working toward new theatrical methods while simultaneously vying for the affections of Nina, an actress in his troupe. The Chekhovian protagonist has a parallel to Williams' own backyard premiers at Bernice Dorothy Shapiro's family garden. Also like Konstantin, Williams was forever enticed by the idea of finding new ways of crafting theatre. Using new types of material and stage conventions, Williams opened several of the windows into what was possible onstage—what Konstantin appeared to be striving for. Where Williams and Konstantin diverge in likeness is that Konstantin lived in the shadow of his mother, Irina Arkadina, a reputable actress, and is lovelorn over Nina. Williams' mother, as surely by now you know, was no kind of freewheeling artiste, and Williams (as far as we know) was never bent on an affair with any of the actors in his plays. Nevertheless, Konstantin's desire to make a symbolic piece of live art closely resembles Williams' "plastic theatre," which he explains in the production note of *The Glass Menagerie,* and which is a ground plan for many of his other plays' dramaturgy.

What we can map is Williams' valuation of character over plot, beginning from his earliest works. His first plays were concerned with situations, but the more masterful he became at his craft, the more personal and interior the action became. Chekhov, even more than Ibsen, was not afraid to sprinkle his plays with only just enough plot points that they weren't static, but he was chiefly interested in crafting distinct, complex portraits of people and their anxieties. Tracing Williams' work from *Cairo! Shanghai! Bombay!* to *Spring Storm,* and beyond to plays like *Menagerie* and *Streetcar,* one can observe fewer plot points but much richer depictions of characters. Moving forward to *Cat* and *Iguana,* this comes into sharper focus, and even more so in his late career with *Tokyo Hotel, Small Craft Warnings,* and the cornucopia of his experimental one-act plays. I assert that it all began in the library that summer, when young Tom Williams introduced himself to Chekhov's writings.

Erwin Piscator and the Family of Expressionism

I tell actors to steal from the best. If they see a delivery or a bit that is brilliant, they should figure out what makes it so successful and use that knowledge to imitate and make it their own. After all, it doesn't work for no reason. Williams said in *Vieux Carré,* in the words of The Writer: "Writers are shameless spies." They write what they know from life, and so every bit of reality they filter into their stories is a piece of hot merchandise. Writers *are* spies. And thieves.

But it isn't theft when it's freely given, is it? That's what happened for Tennessee Williams at the New School in the winter and spring of 1940. The Dramatic Workshop program was a blazing forge bubbling with playwriting mettle in the personages of Tennessee Williams, Arthur Miller, and William Saroyan among others. Exploring style and influences that had impacted their work while turning out experiments in drama at a breakneck speed were some of the activities Williams busied himself with in the workshop. The students were guided by theatrical powerhouse critic John Gassner and German expatriate dramatist/director Erwin Piscator.

I focus on Piscator herein because of his relationship to German Expressionist playwright Bertolt Brecht. Piscator developed with Brecht the Epic style of theatre, which focused on the social and political effects of drama, compared to what they considered vainly artistic or entertaining theatre. In essence, they recognized an additional function that had not been adequately explored in European theatre. Piscator took a working jaunt over to Russia that transformed into an exile when Hitler came to power. Eventually Piscator found himself working in the States, having brought his Epic theatre notions along with a robust appreciation of the Russian acting style.

While in Germany, however, in the good-ish old days before Adolf blew everything to hell, Piscator was a mover and shaker for theatre. In his many endeavors, he attracted the attention of Brecht and was responsible for some of Brecht's formative experiences working in the art form. Brecht carried Piscator's influence with him everywhere he went as he, too, fled the Nazis' growing shadow.

During their time at the New School, Miller and Williams became the other two members of what I consider to be Piscator's tryptic of stylistic sons. Brecht, Miller, and Williams all had considerable differences in style, but they all took conventions in good measure from Piscator, making him perhaps one of the most consequential teachers of theatre in the modern world. Where Williams didn't buy into the idea that formal beauty should be the side dish to social commentary, he did find the idea of the cinematic elements Piscator experimented with thrilling, as did Brecht. Miller didn't go for this so much, but his social themes were highlighted, as were Brecht's; not so much Williams'. Miller and Williams leaned into a more Russian-inspired realism in their dialogue and their idea of how actors should perform, while Brecht's writing (and therefore prescribed performance style) was more presentational; not to say that Williams was never presentational.

Piscator hoped once upon a time to lure Williams over to the more politically controversial side. He tried to convince Williams to make *Battle of Angels* over into a social/political drama, but for Williams, that interpretation didn't resonate. Williams chose instead to keep the personal at the forefront, and relegated the social message of *Battle* to the subtext.

I mention this trapezoidal family tree in my presentation because I feel it's valuable to let readers and audiences know from where a great writer derived inspiration—not just in situations they steal from life, but in the lessons and influences they foster from teachers and peers. I encourage anyone who enjoys Williams to check out plays by Brecht and Miller.

What Is Plastic Theatre?

Did Williams' desire to express kinship with the Chekhov lead him to pick up the character Konstantin's mantel as he drafted up his first several plays? Was Williams conscious as he included bits of Chekhov, Ibsen, and the fictional Konstantin's work as he built his own theatrical vocabulary? Did Gassner and Piscator instill in Williams an aesthetic appreciation for theatrical modes he'd never imagined? The answer to all of these questions is likely "yes."

In the production note for *The Glass Menagerie,* Williams describes a new "plastic theatre." Today, that confuses readers, since our connotation of plastic has become singularly related to a pliable substance used to make bags, kitchen storage, toys, and just about everything else we use—resulting in massive islands of marine-life-killing refuse floating in the oceans. Williams' use of the word meant something else.

Having spent time in Provincetown and other Bohemian circles with artists—particularly sculptors—Williams' definition of "plastic" came to relate to mutable substances formed from unrefined or raw materials. Certainly, in this day and age we relate plastic 100% of the time to the substance, but before the advent of that malleable miracle material, named for its very mutability, plastic meant what Williams understood it to mean.

So, Williams wanted a moldable, re-shapable theatre style. Transformable and transformative. He looked at all of the elements that fit into theatre, from writing to design, acting to stagecraft, and wanted to take each element, rearrange it, reimagine it, and in so doing shape the whole event into something revolutionary. It's done now almost every day, but was radical in Williams' early career.

Looking at *The Glass Menagerie,* we can see Williams putting his sculptor's hands on the method of execution. He explains the use of music, light, and sound effects. He breaks up the action of the play into episodes rather than linear, uninterrupted action, and shows the audience a profile in only the most important moments. Even those moments aren't obviously significant, though; he shows us moments that are emotionally important, not just climactic in the traditional sense. *Menagerie,* which has come to be recognized as a classic example of an easily digested American family drama, was revolutionary in 1944. It was electrifying stage magic. It was a plastic reinvention of the way theatre is executed.

We cannot imagine that Williams' exploration of theatre's plasticity ended with *Menagerie.* He was a mad scientist for much of his career, and even his more down-to-earth plays like *Streetcar, Cat,* and *Summer and Smoke* all feature challenges to the theatrical paradigm. Eventually, theatre caught up to Williams—but his part in redefining the theatrical landscape is undeniable.

But What Do I Do With This Information?

Now that I've regaled you with trivia in regards to Williams' influences and style, you're probably asking yourself the above question. It does seem, after all, to be trivial trivia. *What do I do with this information?* The answer lies in dramaturgy. You may now be asking the follow-up question, "What is a dramaturg?" I'll explain that and how the

Williams "trivia" isn't trivial at all.

In the United States, a dramaturg is often viewed as a glorified theatrical researcher (There are two spellings, "dramaturg" and "dramaturge." I'm using the former; neither is wrong). They are typically tasked with presenting for the director or the team a "world of the play" overview—historical context, events, fashions, perhaps—and an in-depth dramaturgical presentation may even include some social commentary on the mores and attitudes of the day. They may then dive into the life of the playwright, as I have done in the pages of this book, making some connections between true life and stage fiction. That's when many dramaturgs are asked to stop. They must stay in their lanes; not venture into character descriptions or motivations lest they interfere with the actors' or directors' processes.

There is a second, more involved notion of a dramaturg sometimes championed by the more progressive American theatres and by many theatres globally: that the dramaturg is an integral part of the creative team responsible for not just reporting on the world to be put onstage, but being intimately involved in its crafting. In many situations, the director *is* the dramaturg, or *a* dramaturg by trade; like a lighting designer might be an electrician, also. Most technically, the dramaturg in this scenario is tasked with ensuring that all of the symbols, ideas, and story elements harmonize in such a way to elevate one another, crafting a cohesive experience for the audience from the text. This can extend beyond a slideshow about the time period of the play and into the technical elements—use of lights, sound, costumes, properties, set, and media—all the way to the acting conventions—breaking the fourth wall, dance, stylization, blocking. The dramaturg in this scenario keeps the production honest and works to make sure every element jives together with intentionality.

Without an intimate knowledge of the text, a dramaturg is left adrift. They must study the text closely, and in the case of Tennessee Williams, a dramaturg will quickly realize that a full understanding of Williams' biography serves their understanding of any text he put down. You might recall my **detour** way back in Part I about Williams building composite characters from elements of actual figures. That knowledge; a basic awareness of themes and topics explored across multiple Williams plays; influences on his style and dramatic palette; and what elements are based on his biographical life at the time the work was written will aid a dramaturg tremendously. As with all art, an approach rooted in curiosity will bear more captivating outcomes.

Whether it's poems, short stories, essays, or play fragments, we have plenty of extant clues as to the deeper meanings and experiments Williams was conducting at any moment of his career. So, to answer the pressing question (I know you're on pins and needles over this, reader), "What do I do with this information now that I have it?"

Apply it. Know it. Enter a rehearsal room sitting on a foundation of information and enhanced understanding. Do *not*—I repeat, *do not* attempt to show the audience your knowledge, or how much you've studied. I impress this recommendation most strongly. Leave that for biographers and historians. When folks come to see a play, rarely do they want to see the hot dogs being made. They want to enjoy the finished product, maybe with some relish. The crowd doesn't need to see your homework, but trust me when I tell you that they can detect if you've done it . . . or, perhaps more critically, if you *haven't*.

Audiences have a sixth sense for uninformed, incomplete dramaturgy. They may not be able to tell you why they felt a production wasn't cohesive, but they can tell when something was unfinished or "off." Dramaturgy insulates against half-assery that would leave your audience wanting. You may be able to trick and bamboozle them with some razzle dazzle or slapstick, but at the end of the day, audiences can tell with their finely attuned receptors if you haven't done the work. So do it. Do the work . . . but don't make a show of it; they don't like that, either. It's a fine balance, but that's why dramaturgy calls for a unique skill set. Each time you crack a book, though, *you* are one step closer to a more astute dramaturgy about *something*. With this book, it's Tennessee Williams. What's next for you, potential future dramaturg?

Appendix Z

AN UNCOMFORTABLE BUT NECESSARY TREATISE

Diversity in Williams

Tennessee Williams refused to have his plays performed in segregated theatres.

Williams' notion of the "Fugitive Kind" spoke of an overwhelming otherness forced upon people of many different walks of life. The otherness was inflicted upon them, wounding them. They nurse their wounds and remember with their scars in the action of the play. They were the victims of a dominant society, lorded over by a dominant culture. Williams was keenly aware of the politics of exclusion, so it seems silly that exclusive practices be applied when staging his works.

In recent years, there's been a lot more talk about diversity, inclusion, representation, and affirmation. Maybe by the time you're reading this book, if it's had a chance to accumulate some dust and we have finally settled into those flying cars promised in the cartoons of the 1960s, these words and concepts will no longer be novel. Maybe we will be lucky and the vernacular in circulation as I write will one day seem archaic, but the principles of equity they speak to will be culturally enshrined. Perhaps today's *best* practices will be tomorrow's norms. One can hope. Nevertheless, let this addition be a document of the time in which it was written, and a treatise no "101" class—no basic crash course—should be without.

Race in Tennessee Williams plays is treated as untouchable. It needn't be. There are a few plays in which the races of the characters are central to the themes being explored. Most notably in *Sweet Bird of Youth* and *Orpheus Descending,* when the villains are aligned with the white supremacist group the Ku Klux Klan. Sometimes, characters from Latin America are portrayed in an unflattering way by Williams like in *Summer and Smoke* and *Night of the Iguana.* I like to imagine he meant them to be a loving send-up, but if so, it's one that did not age well. Then of course, there's the handling of Sicilian characters, who—when Williams was writing about them—occupied a space of otherness outside of the established white groups of the day (my own family members recalled experiences of being heckled and disparaged for their Sicilian background).

Williams' plays do not exist within an un-racialized vacuum. However, when race is not central to the action, I see no reason to use it as a justification for "historically correct" casting. And yet, as a theatre-maker, I find myself justifying and watching my colleagues have to justify casting Black people in roles.

I'm touching on the topic, of course, of Tennessee Williams' world being a white person's playground. It isn't; it shouldn't be; let's stop that if we haven't already. If Williams' work is to remain as vital, equitable, and universal as I believe he wrote it to be, we must dispense with the idea that the status-owning characters in Williams' plays can only be played by white actors. Or actors without disabilities. Or actors who are cisgender/non-trans. Besides wanting Williams' spirit of inclusivity to be communicated, it's simply the right thing to do. Casts and teams doing Williams' plays need not be as lily-white as those of the 1940s.

Racially non-traditional (read: equitable) casting takes place all the time in classic plays, particularly those in the public domain. For those not accustomed to booking the rights for playmaking, the public domain is free to use, adapt, and present, generally because the authors are long-dead. Williams' plays are not in the public domain as of the publishing of this book.

Sometimes casting is just about who is best for the role. Other times, a more semiotic stance has to be taken. Semiotics is defined as the study of signs and symbols, and their interpretation. You may think of it like semantics—in which a word's meanings are measured against the context in which they're presented, the code being spoken, and such. Only with semiotics, there are no words, per se. Instead, an object presented onstage, onscreen, or so forth, means something because it is a symbol, whether it means to be or not. Images, like words, carry meaning.

Theatre-makers have several considerations when it comes to casting, play selection, hiring, and staging. Sometimes symbols get lost—especially in classics in which the symbols can easily be taken for granted (you wouldn't do Shakespeare's *Othello,* which is concerned with the titular character's race, with an Othello who looks like everyone else; but you might build a Black cast and use a white Othello to highlight the point). It's no different for Tennessee Williams. So here we are at why this becomes relevant to the work of Williams, and why color-conscious casting is a necessary step for the playwright's legacy.

To be able to cast consciously when it comes to any type of diversity is to be aware of the prevailing social narrative in the community in which the work is presented. Having a sensitive director or a dramaturg at the ready to steer a show away from treacherous waters is a foundation for success.

Sometimes, casting can be hyperconscious, such as with stunt casting. Stunt casting is when a director or producer makes a topical casting choice over an appropriate one. Stunt casting is when an actor is selected not because they're right or ideal for the role, but because they're popular, or might be incendiary, or for some other unartistic rationale not rooted in the text. Think of a community theatre production of *A Streetcar Named Desire* where the local grande dame and president of the Ladies' Auxiliary at age fifty is selected to play Blanche—or worse, Stella. That's stunt casting. Imagine if drag queens were really popular in a cultural moment, so a director cast Maggie the Cat with a local drag queen. First, the Williams Estate would not like that very much. Second, it adds layers of queerness that would run right over the nuanced ones Williams put in place, and smacks of sensationalism. Better instead to do a parody one writes oneself, or to do *And Tell Sad Stories of the Deaths of Queens,* which is a Williams play in which a drag queen is the main character.

Stunt casting is rarely the actor's fault (if the actor is cutting a giant check to the production company with an understanding they'll play the role, sure; it is, then). It's usually a tool by a director or a producer in order to jar audiences into buying tickets.

The good news is that increasingly, Williams roles are being cast with diverse performers, and that delights my heart. Knowing that Williams played in *Small Craft Warnings* as Doc in the same run as Candy Darling, a trans woman, I can't imagine

Williams would aim to discriminate based on such characteristics. Were some of his perspectives outdated at the time? Probably. Are many of them outdated now? Certainly. But the spirit of his work was inclusive. That's what's significant.

It cannot be stressed enough that non-minority artists have a head start in just about every conceivable way. Removing that disparity should be the work of anyone putting on a Williams show, since he championed marginalized people. I felt as a theatre-maker and Williams lover that it was my duty to cover this ground because the doors cannot be easily opened from the outside, and it is vitally necessary to let those who have been othered in. In summary, if we expect plays by Williams to be exalted in the same way as plays by Shakespeare, which I think they deserve, the doors to a multicultural society of actors, designers, and storytellers must be open so that they can lay hands on his plays. Williams' plays are American. America is changing—the lens through which we view its playwright's theatre must be checked and adjusted from time to time.

Works of Tennessee Williams

This list, particularly the plays, are the writings of Tennessee Williams that have been produced or published as of 2020. Plays that have been produced but not published are indicated with an asterisk (*). Materials are still being studied and are likely to be published or produced hereafter, but I've striven to produce the most complete list possible. Troves of letters, journal entries, and drafts exist in collections at Harvard, the University of Texas at Austin, The Historic New Orleans Collection, and numerous other places.

Full-length Plays

Battle of Angels
Camino Real
Candles to the Sun
Cat on a Hot Tin Roof
Clothes for a Summer Hotel
The Eccentricities of a Nightingale
Fugitive Kind, The
Glass Menagerie, The
House Not Meant to Stand, A
In the Bar of a Tokyo Hotel
Kingdom of Earth, or The Seven Descents of Myrtle
Kirche, Küche, Kinder (An Outrage for the Stage)
Lovely Sunday for Creve Coeur, A
The Milk Train Doesn't Stop Here Anymore
Mutilated, The
Night of the Iguana, The
Not About Nightingales
Notebook of Trigorin, The
Orpheus Descending

Out Cry
Period of Adjustment
Red Devil Battery Sign, The
Rose Tattoo, The
Small Craft Warnings
Something Cloudy, Something Clear
Spring Storm
Stairs to the Roof
Streetcar Named Desire, A
Suddenly Last Summer
Summer and Smoke
Sweet Bird of Youth
*This Is (An Entertainment)**
Tiger Tail
Two-Character Play, The
Vieux Carré
Will Mr. Merriwether Return from Memphis?
You Touched Me! by Tennessee Williams & Donald Windham

Short Plays (Under 90 minutes, approximately)

27 Wagons Full of Cotton
Adam and Eve on a Ferry
Aimez-vous Ionesco?
And Tell Sad Stories of the Deaths of Queens . . .
At Liberty
Auto-Da-Fé
Beauty Is the Word
Big Game, The
Cairo! Shanghai! Bombay!
Case of the Crushed Petunias, The
Cavalier for Milady, A
Chalky White Substance, The
Confessional
Curtains for the Gentleman
Dark Room, The
Day on Which a Man Dies, The (an Occidental Noh play)
Demolition Downtown, The
Dog Enchanted by the Divine View, The
Enemy: Time, The

Escape
Every Twenty Minutes
Fat Man's Wife, The
Frosted Glass Coffin, The
Gnädiges Fräulein, The
Green Eyes, or *No Sight Would Be Worth Seeing*
Hello from Bertha
Honor the Living
Hot Milk at Three in the Morning
I Can't Imagine Tomorrow
I Never Get Dressed Till After Dark on Sundays
I Rise in Flame, Cried the Phoenix
In Our Profession
Interior: Panic
Ivan's Widow
Jungle, or *Walter Finds the Pearl*
Kingdom of Earth (one-act; there is a full length of the same name)
*Lady from the Village of Falling Flowers, The**
Lady of Larkspur Lotion, The
Last of My Solid Gold Watches, The
Lifeboat Drill
The Long Goodbye, The
Lord Byron's Love Letter
Magic Tower, The
Me, Vashya!
Mister Paradise
Moony's Kid Don't Cry
Municipal Abattoir, The
Night of the Iguana, The (one-act)
Now the Cats with Jeweled Claws
Once in a Lifetime
One Exception, The
Palooka, The
Parade, The, or *Approaching the End of a Summer*
Perfect Analysis Given by a Parrot, A
Pink Bedroom, The
Portrait of a Madonna
Pretty Trap, The (one-act)
Pronoun "I," The (a short work for the lyric theatre)

Purification, The
Reading, The
Recluse and His Guest, A
Remarkable Rooming-House of Mme. LeMonde, The
Sacre de Printemps
Some Problems for Moose Lodge
Something Unspoken
Steps Must Be Gentle
Strange Play, The
Strangest Kind of Romance, The
Summer at the Lake
Sunburst
Taj Mahal with Ink-Wells, The*
Talisman Roses*
Talk to Me Like the Rain and Let Me Listen
Ten Blocks on the Camino Real
Thank You, Kind Spirit
Traveling Companion, The
Unsatisfactory Supper, The
These Are the Stairs You Got to Watch
This Is the Peaceable Kingdom
This Property Is Condemned
Why Do You Smoke So Much, Lily?

Screenplays
All Gaul is Divided
Baby Doll
Loss of a Teardrop Diamond, The
One Arm
Stopped Rocking

Poetry
Collected Poems, The
In the Winter of Cities

Prose
Collected Stories
Hard Candy: A Book of Stories

Memoirs
Moise and the World of Reason
One Arm and Other Stories
Roman Spring of Mrs. Stone, The
Where I Live: New Selected Essays

Letters and Other Personal Writings

Notebooks
Selected Letters of Tennessee Williams, Volume 1, The
Selected Letters of Tennessee Williams, Volume 2, The

Letters and Interviews Included in Volumes by Other Writers

Conversations with Tennessee Williams
*Five O'Clock Angel – Letters of Tennessee Williams to Maria St. Just 1948-1982***
Luck of Friendship, The: The Letters of Tennessee Williams and James Laughlin
Remember Me to Tom by Edwina Williams
Selected Letters of Elia Kazan, The
Tennessee Williams' Letters to Donald Windham, 1940-1965

**Take this with many grains of salt, as St. Just certainly editorialized and fabricated considerable portions of the correspondence.

Bibliography

Books, Interviews, and Essays

Cohn, Ruby. "Tennessee Williams: The Last Two Decades." In *The Cambridge Companion to Tennessee Williams,* edited by Matthew C. Roudané. Cambridge, UK: Cambridge University Press, 1997.

Debusscher, Gilbert. "Creative Rewriting: European and American Influences on the Dramas of Tennessee Williams." In *The Cambridge Companion to Tennessee Williams,* edited by Matthew C. Roudané. Cambridge, UK: Cambridge University Press.

Kazan, Elia. *Kazan on Directing.* New York: Vintage Books, 2009.

Kazan, Elia. *The Selected Letters of Elia Kazan,* edited by Albert J. Devlin and Marlene J. Devlin. New York: Vintage Books, 2016.

Lahr, John, "The Lady and Tennessee." In *Tenn at One Hundred.* Edited by David Kaplan East Brunswick: Hansen Publishing Group, LLC.

Lahr, John. *Tennessee Williams: Mad Pilgrimage of the Flesh.* London: Bloomsbury, 2015.

Leverich, Lyle. *Tom: the Unknown Tennessee Williams.* New York: Crown, 1997.

Maxwell, Gilbert. *Tennessee Williams and Friends.* Cleveland and New York: World Publishing Company, 1965.

Paller, Michael. *Gentlemen Callers.* New York: Palgrave Macmillan, 2005.

Van Gelder, Robert. *Playwright with "A Good Conceit."* In *Conversations with Tennessee Williams,* edited by Albert Devlin. Jackson, MS: University Press of Mississippi, 1986.

Williams, Tennessee. *Memoirs.* New York: New Directions, 2006.

Williams, Tennessee. *Notebooks.* Edited by Margaret Bradham Thornton. New Haven, CT: Yale University Press, 2006.

Williams, Tennessee. *The Selected Letters of Tennessee Williams Volume 1.* Edited by Albert J. Devlin and Nancy Marie Tischler. London: Oberon, 2001.

Williams, Tennessee. *Selected Letters of Tennessee Williams Volume 2*, edited by Albert J. Devlin and Nancy Marie Tischler. New York: New Directions, 2007.

Williams, Tennessee. "Playboy." Interview by C. Robert Jennings. *Conversations with Tennessee Williams.* Edited by Albert Devlin. Jackson, MS: University Press of Mississippi, 1986.

Williams, Tennessee. "Will God Talk Back to a Playwright?" Interview by David Frost. *Conversations with Tennessee Williams.* Edited by Albert Devlin. Jackson, MS: University Press of Mississippi, 1986.

Williams, Tennessee, and Donald Windham. *Tennessee Williams' Letters to Donald Windham, 1940-1965.* Athens, GA: University of Georgia Press, 1996.

Williams, Tennessee, and James Laughlin. *The Luck of Friendship: The Letters of Tennessee Williams and James Laughlin.* Edited by Peggy Fox and Thomas Keith. New York: New Directions, 2018.

Plays Summarized and Referenced

Williams, Tennessee. *27 Wagons Full of Cotton and Other Plays.* New York: New Directions, 1966.

Williams, Tennessee. *Baby Doll & Tiger Tail.* New York: New Directions, 1991.

Williams, Tennessee. *Candles to the Sun.* New York: New Directions, 2004.

Williams, Tennessee. *Camino Real.* New York: New Directions, 2008.

Williams, Tennessee. *Cat on a Hot Tin Roof.* New York: New Directions, 2004.

Williams, Tennessee. *Clothes for a Summer Hotel.* New York: Dramatists Play Services, 1981.

Williams, Tennessee. "The Eccentricities of a

Nightingale." In *The Theatre of Tennessee Williams Volume 2,* 1-112. New York: Dramatists Play Service, Inc., 1971.

Williams, Tennessee. *Fugitive Kind.* New York: New Directions, 2001.

Williams, Tennessee. *The Glass Menagerie.* New York: New Directions, 1999.

Williams, Tennessee. "The Gnädiges Fräulein." In *The Theatre of Tennessee Williams Volume 7,* 219-64. New York: New Directions, 1981.

Williams, Tennessee. *A House Not Meant to Stand.* New York: New Directions, 2008.

Williams, Tennessee. "In the Bar of a Tokyo Hotel." In *The Theatre of Tennessee Williams Volume 7,* 3-58. New York: New Directions, 1981.

Williams, Tennessee. "Kingdom of Earth." In *The Theatre of Tennessee Williams Volume 5,* 121-214. New York, NY: New Directions, 1976.

Williams, Tennessee. *A Lovely Sunday for Creve Coeur.* (New York: New Directions, 1980.

Williams, Tennessee. "The Milk Train Doesn't Stop Here Anymore." In *The Theatre of Tennessee Williams Volume 5,* 1-120. New York: New Directions, 1976.

Williams, Tennessee. "The Mutilated" In *The Theatre of Tennessee Williams Volume 7,* 88-132. New York, NY: New Directions, 1981.

Williams, Tennessee. *Orpheus Descending and Suddenly Last Summer.* New York: New Directions, 2012.

Williams, Tennessee. *The Night of the Iguana.* New York: New Directions, 2009.

Williams, Tennessee. *Not About Nightingales.* New York: New Directions, 1998.

Williams, Tennessee. *Out Cry.* New York: New Directions, 1973.

Williams, Tennessee. "Period of Adjustment" In *The Theatre of Tennessee Williams Volume 4,* 125-246. New York: New Directions, 1972).

Williams, Tennessee. *The Red Devil Battery Sign.* New York: New Directions, 1988.

Williams, Tennessee. *The Rose Tattoo.* New York: New

Directions, 2010.

Williams, Tennessee. *Small Craft Warnings*. New York: New Directions, 1972.

Williams, Tennessee. *Something Cloudy, Something Clear*. New York: New Directions, 1995.

Williams, Tennessee. *Spring Storm*. New York: New Directions, 1999.

Williams, Tennessee. *Stairs to the Roof*. New York: New Directions, 2000.

Williams, Tennessee. "Steps Must Be Gentle." In *Now the Cats with Jeweled Claws & Other One-Act Plays*, 61-70. New York: New Directions, 2016.

Williams, Tennessee. "The Strange Play" In *Now The Cats with Jeweled Claws& Other One-Act Plays*, 173-86. New York: New Directions, 2016.

Williams, Tennessee. *A Streetcar Named Desire*. New York: A New Directions Book, 2004.

Williams, Tennessee. "Summer and Smoke." In *The Theatre of Tennessee Williams Volume 2*, 113-256. New York: New Directions, 1971.

Williams, Tennessee. *Sweet Bird of Youth*. New York: New Directions, 2008.

Williams, Tennessee. *The Two-Character Play*. New York: New Directions, 1976.

Williams, Tennessee. *Vieux Carré*. New York: New Directions, 2000.

Index